D0710022

THE WALL
OF
PARADISE

THE WALL
OF
PARADISE

ESSAYS ON MILTON'S POETICS

JOHN M. STEADMAN

LOUISIANA STATE UNIVERSITY PRESS

BATON ROUGE AND LONDON

Copyright © 1985 by Louisiana State University Press
All rights reserved
Manufactured in the United States of America

Designer: Albert Crochet
Typeface: Linotron Galliard
Typesetter: G & S Typesetters, Inc.

Library of Congress Cataloging in Publication Data

Steadman, John M.
  The wall of paradise.

  Bibliography: p.
  Includes index.
  1. Milton, John, 1608–1674—Aesthetics—Addresses,
essays, lectures.   2. Poetics—Addresses, essays, lectures.
3. Epic poetry—History and criticism—Addresses, essays,
lectures.   I. Title.
PR3592.A34S74   1985   821'.4   85-9671
ISBN 0-8071-1230-5

CONTENTS

PREFACE AND
ACKNOWLEDGMENTS

THE ESSAYS in this volume explore aspects of Milton's poetics in a dual context—the larger framework of Renaissance poetic theory and the narrower but potentially richer context of specific poems, his major epic and his only tragedy. This book is intended to complement earlier studies: *Milton and the Renaissance Hero* (Oxford, 1967); *Milton's Epic Characters: Image and Idol* (Chapel Hill, 1968); and *Epic and Tragic Structure in "Paradise Lost"* (Chicago, 1976).

The first four essays have not been hitherto published Other essays have appeared previously and are reprinted here, with certain changes, by permission.

A fellowship from the John Simon Guggenheim Memorial Foundation, and subsequently a sabbatical leave from the University of California at Riverside, were helpful in assisting me to organize this volume.

To my friends and colleagues at the University of California, Riverside, and at the Henry E. Huntington Library, I am grateful for encouragement in planning this book. To the editors and publishers of the journals or festschrifts in which several of these essays first appeared I am greatly indebted for advice and for permission to reprint.

THE WALL
OF
PARADISE

INTRODUCTION

MILTON ON THE ART OF POETRY

RHETORICAL CONTEXTS

THE DIVERSITY of Renaissance epic and epic theory, and the frequent variance between poetic doctrine and practice, tend to undercut critical and historical generalizations about them. There are usually significant exceptions to most definitions of the traditional poetic genres and styles and to most generalizations concerning the rules and principles governing them. The methods of literary history and criticism may themselves encourage an overemphasis on dubious generalities. In seeking to isolate trends or schools or traditions in the art and literature of the period, in attempting to define the periods themselves and to characterize the predominant period styles, the literary historian, like the historian of culture, is apt to rely on stereotypes. He may inherit his preconceptions of the period and its principal styles and genres from *Geistesgeschichte*, or he may propose other categories of his own invention. Alternatively, he may take the work of a few major poets or critics as normative for the period and its stylistic and generic concepts as a whole. The order that he attempts to impose on the chaos of literary history is usually an order of his own divising or an order valid for a highly restricted number of contemporary artists or theorists. Although he may qualify his stereotypes, distinguishing various subspecies of epic or tragedy and differentiating lesser categories of style or mixtures of style within the principal *genera dicendi*, these concepts may likewise become methodological stereotypes, distorting the concrete data of liter-

1

ary history in subjecting them to an intelligible pattern. The more abstract our generalizations, the more subtle our distinctions, the clearer our definitions of literary categories, and the more logical and consistent our chain of reasoning—the more irrelevant and the more misleading they are sometimes apt to become. Bacon's strictures against Scholastic method in natural history are perhaps equally applicable to the methods of literary history. In the former, the mind was all too prone to anticipate—and thus misconceive—the operations of nature; in the latter, the mind (that enchanted glass) is equally predisposed to anticipate—and misinterpret—the methods of art.

For the student of Renaissance literature, the difficulty is compounded by the fact that many, though by no means all, of the theorists of the period, and a substantial plurality of its poets and orators as well, did in fact accept a normative and idealistic theory of art. They believed in "ideas" (*i.e.*, a priori and universal forms) of the various styles and literary genres—archetypes or exemplars of epic or tragedy or comedy—and formal rules for imitating or embodying these ideal forms. They theorized, disputed, and sometimes composed in terms of stereotypes, even though they frequently disagreed on the definition and extension of these stereotypes, on the rules appropriate to each or all of the ideal genres, and on how rigidly these rules should be applied. The student of Renaissance epic must, accordingly, take into account not only the idealizing tendencies in the theory (and sometimes in the practice) of the period but also the frequent hiatus between theory and practice, and the tendentious exploitation of theory to attack or defend the practice of some particular poet or poetic fashion. He must recognize the variety of contemporary norms or "stereotypes" of heroic poetry during the period, and he must avoid accepting any one of them, or all of them, at face value. He must make due allowance for the idealizing penchant of the age; in assessing its influence, he must be on guard against oversimplifying its critical presuppositions or making its literary norms or stereotypes his own.

MILTON LEFT no systematic poetics, and it would be hazardous to attempt to reconstruct one for him. His scattered remarks on the

2

subject occur in a wide variety of contexts—in political and ecclesiastical treatises, in discourses on education and logic, in occasional headnotes or prefaces to his own poetry, in academic exercises, and in the body of his Latin and English verse. Introduced less for their doctrinal importance than for their argumentative force, less as expositions of poetic theory than as instruments of persuasion, they are often rhetorically conditioned and serve polemical or apologetic ends. Although we should not dismiss them as insincere, we should nevertheless recognize the extent to which they have been influenced by other considerations than a disinterested preoccupation with poetic theory. They have usually been selected for their relevance to a particular argument; they are sometimes tendentious; and the kind of emphasis Milton gives them is frequently relative to his controversial strategy.

Just as biographers have sometimes been led astray by passages of ethical proof in Milton's prose or poetry, students of his critical theory may easily overstress the occasional observations he has made on this subject at the expense of other critical doctrines (perhaps equally important) that he passed over as irrelevant to his immediate rhetorical ends. This is a hazard implicit in historical methodology; we may guard against it, but we cannot altogether avoid it. The methods of the literary historian, like those of the biographer, usually encourage him to rely as far as possible on concrete documentary evidence. Nevertheless, in this instance, the documents available are frequently of dubious evidential value. They belong to diverse literary genres and exhibit variable mixtures of historical fact and poetic fiction, the certainties of the logician, and the probabilities or apparent probabilities of the rhetorician. In evaluating Milton's statements on poetics, we must consider their immediate rhetorical contexts as well as their exploitation of more general rhetorical commonplaces —arguments from expediency or inexpediency, justice or injustice, and honor or shame.

Milton's allusions to the heavenly muse, to the character and discipline of the poet, and to the nature and sources of poetic inspiration, for instance, not only vary with subject and genre but sometimes perform different functions and serve diverse ends. In the *Nativity Ode* his invocation to the celestial muse underlines

3

the sacred character of his theme, but it also reinforces the contrast—developed simultaneously in his elegy (or verse epistle) to Diodati—between higher and lower kinds of poetry, between sacred and secular sources of poetic inspiration, and between spiritual and hedonistic conceptions of the *ethos* requisite for the poet. Subsequently in *A Masque* he mentions the heavenly muse of "sage Poets" (*i.e.*, *vates*) in order to emphasize the divine inspiration underlying the symbolic marvels of pagan and romantic fables—to validate his fable of Circe's son by stressing the moral truths concealed in the ancient myths and to direct his audience to the doctrinal truth concealed under the veil of allegorical fantasy. In this instance, the heavenly muse was, either directly or indirectly, the patroness and preceptress of Gentile bards. Conceivably Milton may have recalled Boccaccio's defense of classical myth, both in the *Life of Dante* and in the *Genealogy of the Gods*, on the grounds that the Gentile mythographers, though not divinely inspired, had nevertheless followed the signs left by the Holy Spirit in the Hebrew Scriptures.[1]

In *The Reason of Church-Government* Milton's emphasis on "devout prayer to that eternal Spirit, who can enrich with all utterance and knowledge" reinforces his argument that poetic abilities are "the inspired gift of God" and possess the "power, beside the office of a pulpit, to imbreed and cherish in a great people the seeds of virtue and public civility."[2] In *Paradise Lost* his allusions to his muse not only underline the distinction between divine and secular poetry and between biblical truth and Gentile fable but also exploit the conventional topics of *honestas* (or nobility) common in Renaissance encomia or apologies for a particular art or science—its antiquity, its noble origin, and the nobility of its ends and its subject matter. Urania, or the muse of divine poetry, existed, he declares, *before* the creation of the world; her origin is celestial, and her purposes and subject matter are heavenly. The argument from etymology (*i.e.*, Urania, "heavenly") is likewise a traditional topic of encomium, the *argumentem à nomine*.

1. See the discussion of this point in *Milton Encyclopedia*, ed. William B. Hunter, Jr., *et al.* (Lewisburg, Pa., 1978–), s.v. "Urania."
2. John Milton, *The Reason of Church-Government Urged Against Prelaty*, in *Complete Poems and Major Prose*, ed. Merritt Y. Hughes (New York, 1957), 669.

Finally, in Book IV of *Paradise Regained* the contrast that Milton draws between the sources of Greek and Hebrew poetry—"Such are from God inspir'd, not such from thee"—is conditioned by the antithesis, fundamental to the second temptation and indeed to the entire poem, between human and divine or worldly and heavenly powers. The poets and orators and philosophers of Greece represent the wisdom of a perverted world, just as the Parthian armies represent its strength, and the Roman imperium its political authority and dominion. The hero of Milton's poem is himself "the power and wisdom of God"; and it is inevitable that he should reject the wisdom of the world just as he rejects its military might and its political dominion.[3] Milton does leave unresolved the question of how far the poets and sages of Greece may have been influenced "By light of Nature, not in all quite lost," but theirs is nevertheless merely the wisdom and eloquence of nature, not of grace.

Like his early reference to the abstinence demanded of the poet as *vates*, in the elegy to Diodati, Milton's later allusions to the inner illumination of the blind *vates*, both in *Paradise Lost* and in the *Second Defence*, serve as ethical proof. In the epic this *topos* reinforces the "metaphor of inspiration" (to borrow John T. Shawcross' phrase) and the imagery of intellectual and spiritual vision and poetic *ecstasis*, or rapture. At the same time it further strengthens the correlation between the *ethos* of the poet and the nature of the illumination and inspiration that he receives from his celestial guide.[4] In the *Defence*, similarly, he adroitly exploits the *topos* of the blind *vates* to rebut the calumnies of his enemies and to turn their arguments against themselves. Countering the charge that his blindness was a divine punishment inflicted upon him for his sacrilegious defamation of the sacred memory of King Charles I, he associates his own affliction with the blindness of inspired sages and heroic patriots. He stresses the divine cause and the di-

3. Compare I Cor. 1.24, "Christ the power of God, and the wisdom of God."
4. For Milton's use of ethical proof, see John S. Diekhoff, "The Function of the Prologues in *Paradise Lost*," *PMLA*, LVII (1942), 697–704, and *Milton's "Paradise Lost": A Commentary on the Argument* (New York, 1946); John T. Shawcross, "The Metaphor of Inspiration in *Paradise Lost*," in Amadeus P. Fiore (ed.), *Th' Upright Heart and Pure* (Pittsburgh, 1967), 75–85.

vine occasion for his loss of sight. He emphasizes the signs of divine favor and the interior light that "irradiate" his darkness, and he represents himself (in implicit contrast to the royal martyr) as a person almost "too sacred to attack."

In the same way, Milton's emphasis on chastity in his *Apology for Smectymnuus*—chastity in lyric and romantic poetry, in philosophy and Scripture, and in the life and writings of the ideal poet—is rhetorically conditioned by the personal slanders of his adversary. His "digression," as he himself terms it, on his poetic ambitions in *The Reason of Church-Government* likewise serves as ethical proof. As part of an extended exordium to the second book of his treatise, it reinforces his argument that he has taken up his pen on the controversial and unpopular theme of prelatry not through personal ambition but in obedience to the divine dictates of conscience. This is, he insists, an uncongenial undertaking, for he is "led by the genial power of nature to another task," and in this "manner of writing" he knows "myself inferior to myself," having "the use . . . but of my left hand." If he had "hunted after praise by the ostentation of wit and learning, [he] should not write thus out of mine own season"; and if he "were wise only to mine own ends, [he] would certainly take such a subject as of itself might catch applause, whereas this hath all the disadvantages on the contrary." His digression on his poetic hopes and plans serves to "make it manifest with what small willingness I endure to interrupt the pursuit of no less than these." There can be no honor in dealing "against such adversaries"; but "were it the meanest underservice, if God by his secretary conscience should enjoin it, it were sad for me if I should draw back." From this argument, finally, Milton turns to an additional proof of his "right . . . to meddle in these matters"—the fact that he had been destined from childhood for the ministry, but was subsequently "church-outed by the prelates."[5]

Since *The Reason of Church-Government* provides the most extensive and most detailed account of Milton's views on poetry and of his own poetic ambitions, it is indispensable for any study of his

5. Milton, *The Reason of Church-Government*, in *Complete Poems and Major Prose*, 665–71.

poetic theory. To utilize it effectively as evidence, however, the literary historian and the biographer alike must take into account its polemical context. The digression on poetry not only attempts to justify the author's "meddling," to argue the nobility and disinterestedness of his motives, and to depreciate the quality of his opponents; it also emphasizes the magnitude of the evil he is attacking and the urgency of the problem. If poetry can be so beneficial to church and state, a reader might legitimately ask, why—in the name of common sense—does the poet not exercise his right hand in celebrating the "throne and equipage of God's almightiness" and the "victorious agonies of martyrs and saints" instead of shaking croziers, smiting miters, and jabbing prelates with his left? The implicit answer is that Milton is writing *not* in the name of common sense but in God's name and in God's cause. When "God commands to take the trumpet and blow a dolorous or a jarring blast, it lies not in man's will what he shall say or what he shall conceal." The "cause of God and his church was to be pleaded, for which purpose that tongue was given thee which thou hast." The immediate "tribulations of the church," he is arguing, temporarily outweigh the future civil and religious benefits that he might confer through his poetry. Conscience and "a preventive fear" of sins of omission have constrained the dedicated poet to this uncongenial and unpopular task. In fostering and communicating this sense of urgency, Milton compares himself to Jeremiah—"His word was in my heart as a burning fire shut up in my bones"—but as he well knew, it was also a well-established satiric convention. In classical, medieval, and Renaissance literature alike, the satirist represents himself as constrained to speak the truth in spite of the dictates of prudence and self-interest—compelled by the magnitude of contemporary evils and by his own conscience or his moral indignation.

Although one need not doubt Milton's sincerity, one should not underestimate his rhetorical art. In the context of a treatise on ecclesiastical government and on the relationship between church and state, it was clearly to his advantage to emphasize the public offices of poetry, its scriptural precedents, its "doctrinal," "exemplary," and "persuasive" functions, and its utility to the commonwealth in maintaining the true principles of morality, politics, and religion.

Milton's brief account of poetics in *Of Education* is significant primarily for its fidelity to the theory of genres and the "laws" governing each of the literary kinds, its emphasis on decorum and on the "religious . . . and magnificent" use of poetry in both "divine and human things," and for its catalog of authorities on this "sublime art"—Aristotle's *Poetics*, Horace's *Ars Poetica*, and the "Italian commentaries of Castelvetro, Tasso, Mazzoni, and others." There is, however, comparatively little evidence for Milton's poetic doctrine. The authors have been chosen for their potential merit as school texts—books which can teach the rules and precepts for the different poetic genres. Most of these authors are frequently at variance with one another on issues of fundamental importance, and Milton does not discuss their contradictions.[6] Moreover, this list of authorities is incomplete. It does not include Piccolomini or Scaliger or Minturno, Vida or Robortello or Heinsius, Jonson or Sidney—all of whom he may have known. (His reference in *The Reason of Church-Government* to "those dramatic constitutions, wherein Sophocles and Euripides reign," may conceivably echo the title of Heinsius' influential treatise *De Tragoediae Constitutione*.) Finally, we do not know how well he knew these authorities or precisely how he would have ranked the later authors in relation to one another and to the numerous authors he has (for the sake of conciseness, if nothing more) left unnamed. The fact that he cites no authorities on logic and mentions neither Ramus nor Talaeus among his texts on rhetoric tends to diminish the value of his catalog of *artes poeticae* as an index of his own poetic doctrine.[7]

6. Milton, *Of Education*, in *ibid.*, 636–37.

7. For the possible influence of Daniel Heinsius' tragic theory on Milton, see Paul R. Sellin, "Sources of Milton's Catharsis: A Reconsideration," *Journal of English and Germanic Philology*, LX (1961), 712–30, "Milton and Heinsius: Theoretical Homogeneity," in Rosario P. Armato and John M. Spalek (eds.), *Medieval Epic to the "Epic Theater" of Brecht* (Los Angeles, 1968), 125–34, and *Daniel Heinsius and Stuart England* (Leiden, 1968); Daniel Heinsius, *On Plot in Tragedy*, trans. Paul R. Sellin and John J. McManmon (Northridge, Calif., 1971). See also Martin Mueller, "Sixteenth-Century Italian Criticism and Milton's Theory of Catharsis," *Studies in English Literature*, VI (1966), 139–50; John Arthos, "Milton and the Passions: A Study of *Samson Agonistes*," *Modern Philology*, LXIX (1972), 209–21.

The position of poetics in Milton's educational scheme reflects, in fact, his dual emphasis on the primacy of things over words and on the methodical arrangement of the arts in order of increasing difficulty. As in the "education of Adam" in *Paradise Lost*, the understanding must found itself "on sensible things," arriving at knowledge of things invisible "by orderly conning over the visible and inferior creature." Language is merely "the instrument conveying to us things useful to be known." A linguist must study "the solid things" in the tongues he masters "as well as the words and lexicons." [8]

Accordingly, the organic arts—logic, rhetoric, and poetics— are placed last in Milton's curriculum. Although his hypothetical students have already studied Greek and Latin poetry, they have read it first and foremost for its content—natural history, agriculture, economics or "household matters," ethics, and politics. Having mastered *things*, they may proceed to the mastery of *words*. They may now take up the organic (*i.e.*, "instrumental") arts which "enable men to discourse and write perspicuously, elegantly, and according to the fitted style of lofty, mean, or lowly." [9] Among these, logic comes first—significantly, Milton discusses it primarily in terms of the *loci communes*, or commonplaces, for inventing or finding arguments. For Aristotle, this had belonged properly to dialectics, though he had also discussed in detail the rhetorical topics of invention. Cicero had devoted his *Topica* to this matter, and for humanist educators, the invention of rhetorical arguments was closely associated with the notebook-and-heading method and the compilation of commonplace books as a source of *copia rerum* ("abundance of matter" or "things"). Ramus and his followers, in turn, had assigned the invention and disposition of arguments to dialectics (or logic), leaving style (diction and verbal adornment) and delivery to the art of rhetoric. For humanist educators, style, or *elocutio*, involved close study and imitation of classical authors of the "best" period, with the assistance of lexicons, manuals of synonyms and epithets, and other aids to *copia verborum* ("abundance of words"). [10]

---

8. Milton, *Of Education*, in *Complete Poems and Major Prose*, 631–32.
9. *Ibid.*, 636–37.
10. On *loci communes*, *res et verba*, and *copia rerum et verborum*, see Ruth Mohl, *John*

Just as the position of the organic arts in his curriculum reflects Milton's emphasis on the priority of things over words, and of sound knowledge over verbal style, the primary position that he assigns logic among the organic arts indicates his belief in the priority of the invention of matter over its expression and adornment in words. Only after the student has mastered the "well-couched heads and topics" of logic—has acquired a knowledge of the commonplaces of invention and achieved a *copia rerum*—can he proceed to a "graceful and ornate rhetoric." *Copia verborum*, in short, must be subsequent to *copia rerum*. Poetry, in turn, is subsequent to rhetoric—"or indeed rather precedent, as being less subtle and fine, but more simple, sensuous, and passionate." At this stage— "from hence, and not till now"—the students may engage in *praxis*, in actual literary composition. This will be "the right season of forming them to be able writers and composers in every excellent matter, when they shall be thus fraught with an universal insight into things."[11]

The position of the organic arts in this scheme is interesting not only for its bearing on the long-standing controversy over the relative importance and priority of *res* and *verba* but also for the roughly analogous position that the rhetoric and poetry of Greece would occupy in the sequence of temptations in *Paradise Regained*. In assessing the value of Milton's account of poetics in *Of Education* for his own theory and practice, one must bear in mind its limited and highly restricted scope. He is not writing an *ars poetica*—or even an ideal scheme for the education of a poet, comparable to Cicero's and Quintilian's treatises on the education of an orator. Poetry, like rhetoric, is merely one of numerous arts essential for the "complete and generous education" which can fit "a man to perform . . . all the offices, both private and public, of peace and war."[12]

Milton and His Commonplace Book (New York, 1969); R. R. Bolgar, *The Classical Heritage and Its Beneficiaries from the Carolingian Age to the End of the Renaissance* (New York, 1964); Ernst Robert Curtius, *European Literature and the Latin Middle Ages*, trans. Willard R. Trask (New York, 1963).

11. Milton, *Of Education*, in *Complete Poems and Major Prose*, 636–37.
12. *Ibid.*, 632.

10

Moreover, the scheme of instruction that he outlines is, in many respects, very different from the kind of education that he and many other pupils of Renaissance humanists had received. Despite its heavily classical curriculum, his program of instruction is not exclusively (and barely primarily) literary. The study of rhetoric and poetics occurs *last* in the sequence of the arts; and actual composition or *praxis* is deferred until a still later "season." The intimate correlation between the study of art or precepts, close reading of classical texts, and actual composition (including imitation of classical models)—which was characteristic of Quintilian's method and that of many of the Renaissance humanist educators—is significantly missing in Milton's scheme. The elements are there, but they have been rearranged and dispersed. A student in Milton's ideal academy would not have received the same kind of education that Milton had received at Saint Paul's School, nor would he have studied the principles of rhetoric and poetics and the works of classical authors by the same method and sequence that Milton himself had studied them.

Milton's allusion to unity of action as a "rule" of epic poetry, in the *Second Defence*, is introduced specifically to heighten the exploits of the English revolutionaries by likening them to the *aristeia* of epic heroes and to enhance the gravity of his panegyric on Cromwell and other English worthies by comparing it to heroic poetry. His defense of their exploits is, he "would almost say," a "monument that will not readily be destroyed to the reality of those singular and mighty achievements which were above all praise." Like the epic poet who, observing the "rules of that species," celebrates one particular action of a hero, Milton himself has "heroically celebrated at least one exploit of my countrymen." He must "pass by the rest, for who could recite the achievements of a whole people?" The reference to the rules of epic poetry in this passage is instrumental to the author's "justification or apology" for his encomium of deeds that transcend encomia. Finally, it serves as a *suasoria*, a hortatory argument urging his countrymen to complete the heroic enterprise that they had so gloriously begun and offering the additional stimulus of the immortality of fame conferred by literary eloquence—by the voice of an orator

11

who is also, or still aspires to be, a heroic poet. His countrymen (if they fail) will not only "see that there was a rich harvest of glory and an opportunity afforded for the greatest achievements," they will also perceive that men—like Milton himself—"were not wanting who could rightly counsel, exhort, inspire, and bind an unfading wreath of praise round the brows of the illustrious actors in so glorious a scene."[13]

The censure of pagan poetry, in *Paradise Regained*, in turn, is based not only on moral and religious principles but also on poetic criteria—the demands of decorum and verisimilitude in characterization. These literary criteria, however, are partly contingent on ethical and theological norms. Like the Greek philosophers, the Gentile poets are ignorant of the true God, of the fallen condition of man, and of the true principles of morality and religion. They have imitated badly the arts that they had borrowed from the Hebrews, lauding the illaudable and celebrating their own vices and the vices of their deities. Hence they have made their gods appear ridiculous, "and themselves past shame." Their poems, "Thin sown with aught of profit or delight," violate the conventional ends of poetry—the combination of *utile* and *dulce* that Horace demanded of the superior poet.

Although this passage may seem inconsistent with the praise that Milton elsewhere bestows on classical epic, lyric, and tragedy—and on classical poetic theory—we must guard against detaching it from its immediate context. Milton is arguing the superiority of the revealed word of God to merely human wisdom and eloquence and exalting the heavenly wisdom and divine poetry of the biblical revelation (including the unwritten as well as the written word) over their secular counterparts. He is extolling the doctrinal truth and "majestic unaffected style" of the Scriptures—and, more significantly, the simplicity of the gospel itself—over the vain philosophy of the world and the lying fables of the Gentiles. Within this specific context his argument is valid and relevant; but it would clearly be out of place in other contexts, such as the preface to *Samson Agonistes* or the defense of unrhymed

13. Milton, *Second Defence*, in *Complete Poems and Major Prose*, 838.

verse inserted (retrospectively) into later issues and editions of *Paradise Lost*.

Milton added his note "The Verse" to his major epic in response to a request from his publisher to remove the *scandalon* that had "stumbled" many of the poem's first readers—"why the Poem Rimes not." Its context and intent are clearly apologetic, as is the preface to his drama. Unlike most of his contemporaries—or indeed the majority of Renaissance dramatists—Milton had followed the Greek model in structuring his tragic plot. In defense of this unfamiliar and unfashionable pattern, he extols the dignity and utility of tragedy composed according to the ancient (*i.e.*, Hellenic) model and praises Aeschylus, Sophocles, and Euripides as "the best rule to all who endeavor to write Tragedy."

Despite the diverse contexts in which they occur, Milton's allusions to the art of poetry indicate, on the whole, a respect for the tradition of Aristotelian and Horatian theory and for the imitation of major works as models. This is, in fact, consistent with his humanistic training in *ars*, *imitatio*, and *praxis*.[14] In addition, however, his longer sketches for tragedies on biblical themes employ technical terms derived from Terentian criticism. He utilizes the term *epitasis*, which had entered Renaissance literary criticism through the tradition of Donatus and Evanthius; and at a climactic moment in the action of *Samson Agonistes*, he inserts a literal translation of *summa epitasis*, or the point of highest tension. This term, derived primarily from comic theory, had nevertheless been introduced into the criticism of tragedy and thus integrated with the Aristotelian-Horatian tradition.[15] Other technical terms, such

14. See Donald Lemen Clark, *Milton at St. Paul's School* (New York, 1948).

15. For the terms *protasis, epitasis, summa epitasis,* and *catastrophe*, see T. W. Baldwin, *Shakspere's Five-Act Structure* (Urbana, 1963); Marvin T. Herrick, *Comic Theory in the Sixteenth Century* (Urbana, 1964); Bernard Weinberg, *A History of Literary Criticism in the Italian Renaissance* (2 vols.; Chicago, 1961); Maria Wickert, "Miltons Entwürfe zu einem Drama vom Sündenfall," *Anglia*, LXXIII (1955), 171–206; Walther Schork, *Die Dramenpläne Miltons* (Freiburg im Breisgau, 1934). For the identification of the argument of a poem with its plot (*mythos, fabula, constitutio rerum, systasis,* or *ton pragmaton synthesis*), see Herrick, *Comic Theory*, 93–94. For the similar application of the rhetorical terms *dispositio, ordo,* and *oeconomia* (denoting the "orderly disposal of the various parts of a discourse") to the structure of incidents in the comic or tragic plot, see *ibid.*, 94–106. For *parasceve* ("preparation, specifically the artful linking of scenes together"),

as *prologue* and *catastrophe*, also belonged to the tradition of Terentian commentary; in the Aristotelian poetic tradition, however, the term *prologos* bore a different sense.[16]

Certain critical studies have done much to illuminate the affinities between Milton's treatment of the several poetic genres and Italian theory and practice; even though the main outlines of his own *ars poetica* (if indeed he ever formulated one) may remain as elusive as ever, further investigation of Renaissance poetic treatises, epics and tragedies and lyrics, and commentaries on classical poetry should enable us to see the technical problems encountered by a late Renaissance heroic and tragic poet more or less through contemporary eyes—and to evaluate the craftsmanship of *Paradise Lost* in a specifically Renaissance context.[17]

in *oeconomia*, see *ibid.*, 102. Milton alludes to the epitasis of "Moabitides or Phineas" and of "Abias Thersaeus," to the prologue of "Paradise Lost" and "Baptistes," and to the "oiconomie" of "Abram from Morea, or Isack redeemd" in his dramatic sketches in the Trinity manuscript (*The Works of John Milton* [New York, 1938], XVIII, 229, 232, 235, 237, 240). Compare his references to "Prologue" in the preface to *Samson Agonistes* and his allusion to "the Catastrophe" in "The Argument" to the same poem.

16. For the different meanings of *prologue* in Aristotle's *Poetics* and in the tradition of Evanthius-Donatus, see T. W. Baldwin and S. H. Butcher, *Aristotle's Theory of Poetry and Fine Art* (4th ed.; New York, 1951), 42–43. Butcher translates Aristotle's phrase *teleutosa ex enantias* as "catastrophe" (46–47). The word *catastrophe* does not occur in Aristotle's *Poetics* (Aristotle, *On the Art of Poetry*, ed. and trans. Ingram Bywater [Oxford, 1909], 373–74).

17. For discussion of Milton's apparent indebtedness to Italian (and other Continental or British) conceptions of epic, tragedy, satire, and certain lyric genres (the sonnet, the *canzone*, the Pindaric ode), see the following studies: John S. Smart (ed.), *The Sonnets of Milton* (Glasgow, 1921); F. T. Prince, *The Italian Element in Milton's Verse* (Oxford, 1954); Robert Beum, "So Much Gravity and Ease," in Ronald David Emma and John T. Shawcross (eds.), *Language and Style in Milton* (New York, 1967), 333–68; Joseph Anthony Wittreich, Jr., *Visionary Poetics: Milton's Tradition and His Legacy* (San Marino, Calif., 1979); Clay Hunt, *"Lycidas" and the Italian Critics* (New Haven and London, 1979); Edward Weismiller, "The Dry and Rugged Verse," in Joseph H. Summers (ed.), *Lyric and Dramatic Milton* (New York and London, 1965), 115–52; Sellin, "Sources of Milton's Catharsis," 712–30; Martin E. Mueller, *"Pathos* and *Katharsis* in *Samson Agonistes," ELH,* XXXI (1964), 156–74; Sherman H. Hawkins, "Samson's Catharsis," *Milton Studies,* II (1970), 211–30; Irene Samuel, *Dante and Milton: The "Commedia" and "Paradise Lost"* (Ithaca, 1966), "Milton on Comedy and Satire," *Huntington Library Quarterly,* XXXV (1972), 107–30, *"Samson Agonistes* as Tragedy," in Joseph Anthony Wittreich, Jr. (ed.), *Calm of Mind: Tercentenary Essays on "Paradise Regained" and "Samson Agonistes" in Honor of John S. Diekhoff* (Cleveland and London, 1971), 235–57, *"Paradise Lost* as Mimesis," in C. A. Patrides (ed.), *Approaches to "Paradise Lost"* (London, 1968), 15–29.

1

NOTES FOR AN *ARS POETICA*

THE OFFICE OF THE POET

MILTON'S CONCEPTION of the office of the poet reflects the synthetic tradition of sixteenth-century Italian criticism. On the one hand, it unites Horatian and Aristotelian "laws" for the art of poetry with humanistic ideals concerning the relationship of eloquence to moral and civil philosophy. Yet it also reflects traditional Christian conceptions (inherited from patristic and medieval doctrine but sharpened by Reformation and Counter Reformation literary and artistic criticism) of the subordination of the arts to the ends of religion, to the demands of faith and devotion. Like many other humanists, Milton retained the idealistic conception of eloquence advanced in Plato's *Phaedrus* and elaborated by Cicero and Saint Augustine. Discourse was the garment of thought, portraying universals through particulars. By investing the invisible forms of the virtues with sensuous forms, eloquence could make them appear amiable and desirable; it could simultaneously teach, delight, and move. Accordingly, it might serve as the instrument of church and state, persuading to virtue and to the invisible objects of faith and worship.

Like many Renaissance poetic theorists, Milton combined Horace's emphasis on the poetic exemplar, which could teach more effectively than the precepts of Chrysippus and Crantor or of Scotus and Aquinas, with Aristotle's stress on the universal as the object of the poet's imitation. Like the Italian theorists of the late Cinquecento, he united the Horatian doctrine of utility and delight (*utile* and *dulce*, or *prodesse* and *delectare*) with Aristotle's views on the special delight conferred by imitation and the special utility resulting from the purgation of the passions. Like his contemporaries and near-contemporaries, he conceived the art of poetry as a system of laws and rules. He too recognized the distinctions among the several literary genres. He too stressed the principle of decorum, "the grand masterpiece to observe." He too acknowledged the authority of the ancients in providing "rules" and "models" for correct imitation. Nevertheless he also felt free to doubt (in *The Reason of Church-Government*) whether "the rules of Aristotle herein are strictly to be kept, or nature to be followed" and to propose modern and biblical compositions as well as classical poems as potential models.

To "imitate those magnific odes and hymns" of Pindar and Callimachus was to follow Horace's advice concerning close study of the Greek masterpieces. It also meant fidelity to the humanistic principle of judicious and selective imitation—for Milton was fully aware that Pindar and Callimachus were "in most things worthy," but that "some others [were] in their frame judicious, in their matter most an[d] end faulty." To teach over "the whole book of sanctity and virtue through all the instances of example with such delight to those especially of soft and delicious temper who will not so much as look upon Truth herself, unless they see her elegantly dressed" was an ideal reminiscent of Horace's principle of combined utility and delight. Nevertheless, it also recalls the Ciceronian (and humanistic) principle of fostering the love of virtue by investing the virtues with amiable forms. The "persuasive method" of uniting popular "recreation and instruction" in theaters and porches and the proposal to sweeten "wise and artful recitations . . . with eloquent and graceful enticements to the love and practice" of the virtues reflect the traditional ends of humanistic rhetorical theory and Horatian poetics. Milton's emphasis on the power of poetry to "allay the perturbations of the mind and set the affections in right tune" and his reference to "whatsoever hath passion or admiration in all the changes of that which is called fortune from without, or the wily subtleties and refluxes of man's thoughts from within" demonstrate his direct or indirect indebtedness to classical poetic and rhetorical theory. His stress on the "divine argument" of scriptural poetry and its excellence in "the very critical art of composition" echoes the arguments of contemporary apologists for "divine poetry." This insistence on the poet's abilities "to celebrate in glorious and lofty hymns the throne and equipage of God's almightiness, and what he works and what he suffers to be wrought with high providence in his church, to sing the victorious agonies of martyrs and saints, the deeds and triumphs of just and pious nations doing valiantly through faith against the enemies of Christ, to deplore the general relapses of kingdoms and states from justice and God's true worship" recalls the aesthetic ideals of the Reformation and Counter-Reformation.[1]

In its basic concepts—and in its ethical, political, and religious orientation—Milton's poetic theory is conventional and conservative. Its principal foundations are fourfold: first, the humanistic conception of eloquence as an instrument of moral education (like its sister arts, rhetoric and painting, poetry is useful to the commonweal as an instrument of moral education, teaching and persuading delightfully through examples just as rhetoric teaches and persuades through enthymemes); second, the Horatian ends of profit and delight; third, Aristotle's discussion of imitation and catharsis, as interpreted by several generations of critics in light of the Horatian tradition; fourth, the Reformation and Counter-Reformation emphasis on poetry as an instrument of faith and devotion.

In view of the scarcity of evidence, it is difficult to demonstrate a pattern of development in Milton's critical thought. His own literary education had been classical; his principal authorities on poetics and rhetoric were classical writers or modern commentators on classical writers. Not surprisingly, his own theory was predominantly neoclassical, but it was not, on the whole, rigid or uncompromising. When he wrote *The Reason of Church-Government*, his doctrine was sufficiently flexible to accommodate the method

---

1. John Milton, *The Reason of Church-Government Urged Against Prelaty*, in *Complete Poems and Major Prose*, ed. Merritt Y. Hughes (New York, 1957), 665–71.

of nature as well as the rules of Aristotle. If one compares that passage with his later statement, in the *Second Defence*, concerning the rules of the epic species, one may detect an increasingly Aristotelian and neoclassical bias; the evidence, however, is far too flimsy to support this inference. Although the preface to *Samson Agonistes* exhibits a high esteem for Aristotle's authority, it nevertheless recommends the actual dramas of the three major Greek tragedians as the "best rule" for writing tragedy—not the *Poetics* of Aristotle or Castelvetro's exhaustive commentary. Christ's summary dismissal of Greek poetry in *Paradise Regained*, on the other hand, appears to undercut the value of these and other classical authors as models for imitation and rules for composition.

To detach these (and other) observations on poetics from their original contexts, piecing them together like mosaic fragments in an attempt to reconstruct a systematic poetic doctrine or, alternatively, a coherent pattern of development and change in Milton's poetics, is a dangerous procedure. To a certain extent, however, it is an inevitable, though regrettable, necessity. If we are to take account of apparent contradictions or discrepancies in Milton's critical statements, we must either assume that he had altered his beliefs or else attempted to reconcile them by introducing Scholastic distinctions and qualifications or by seeking further (albeit hypothetical) principles to explain the inconsistencies. In either case, we are apt to project a pattern of our own making on Milton's thought.

It is likely that Milton's views on poetics and rhetoric altered, as did his literary tastes, during his long lifetime—developing as his poetic ambitions and his command of his medium matured—but we do not possess sufficient evidence to reconstruct these changes. The most satisfactory evidence is the indirect testimony of his poetry; in this case, the problem is complicated by the demands of different genres. The testimony itself is sometimes ambiguous, and in interpreting it, one is sometimes apt to impose an extrinsic pattern arbitrarily on the text rather than to abstract the form of the poet's own design.

Many of the apparent inconsistencies are merely superficial and reflect different emphases rather than divergences in doctrine. Insofar as the end of theory was practice, and the practice of art partly conditioned by the poet's native ability, or *ingenium*, the rules of art tended to be flexible. An *ars poetica* was not the sole arbiter of taste or the only guide to composition. In most humanistic programs of instruction, art (conceived as a systematic body of general precepts or rules) was merely one of several factors that might receive virtually the same emphasis. It was scarcely more important than close study and imitation of specific models. In the literary education of a Renaissance schoolboy, art, imitation, and exercise were conceived as correlative and complementary disciplines, as closely interlinked as the Graces themselves. In emphasizing the study and imitation of classical models as well as the precepts of classical poetic theory—and in perfecting his own technical skill through exercising his craft in a variety of genres, progressing (like Virgil and Spenser) by gradual but regular stages from easier to more difficult forms—Milton was faithful to the principles of his humanistic schooling. There is no inconsistency between his veneration for the "sublime art" taught by Aristotle and Horace and his belief that the classical poets themselves constituted the "best rule" for writing tragedy.

Nor, on the other hand, is the censure of classical poetry in *Paradise Regained* inconsistent with his imitation of classical models. As in his earlier criticism of certain lyric poets, his censure is directed not so much against the form or design of classical poetry as against its matter and end. The primary grounds—in this instance, at least—are its source of inspiration; and this is peculiarly relevant to the theme of Milton's "brief epic" and to the identity of its protagonist and antagonist, the incarnate Logos and the prince of a fallen world. As Truth itself, the living oracle and manifested Word of God, the hero of the poem is himself the channel and agent of divine wisdom and divine inspiration, and he must inevitably reject the products of an inferior source of inspiration, contaminated by sin or at best faintly illuminated by the light of nature. As the "true light," the prophet whose mission is to "instruct his church in heavenly truth, and to declare the whole will of his father" both through the external "promulgation of divine truth" and through the internal "illumination of the understanding," he cannot, without contradicting his own nature, seek instruction and solace from profane poets—*vates* inspired by a lesser muse and illuminated by a lesser light. In the trial of his obedience to the Father, it is essential that he rely consistently on divine inspiration and guidance, on the scriptural word of God and on the inner motions of the Spirit. The Spirit who leads him into the desert and brings him thence "By proof th'undoubted Son of God" is the same Spirit who inspires Milton's own "prompted Song." This is the true source of divine poetry; and Milton's divine *vates* must inevitably reject the secular eloquence of poets inspired by no heavenly muse.

The pedagogical tradition in which Milton had been educa¹ had usually emphasized the formal precepts of art, the close study and imitation of models, and frequent literary exercises. These were not only complementary and interrelated; they were also subject to cross-influences. The rules of art as well as personal taste and *ingenium* might condition the writer's choice of models and the particular points he chose to imitate or adapt—or indeed to ignore or parody or censure. Imitation, as Quintilian had taught, must be selective and judicious—more than slavish copying. The apprentice's close study of major authors, in turn, could lead him to modify and qualify the theories of the *artes poeticae* he had studied. In varying degrees perhaps, both of these factors would condition his own practice; nevertheless, his own exercises might reciprocally affect his conception of the principles of art and his estimate of the authors he had studied. Some precepts would appear more practical and more valid than other critical doctrines. Certain features in a particular author would seem more useful and more imitable than others. One cannot, it seems, define Milton's poetic theory, or the changes in it, without reference to his practice and to the classical or modern authors whom he studied and imitated. On the other hand, one cannot evaluate his literary imitations or adaptations without reference to his *ars poetica* and his *ars rhetorica*. To consider the influence of his poetics on his actual poetry, one must simultaneously take into account the influence of particular models or of traditional literary formulas and motifs. This synthetic approach may easily result in

20

circular reasoning—like that of Boethius' Philosophy—but the alternative approaches are likely to be too narrow. They may offer an easier and more practical method, but this technical advantage is often offset by their restricted scope.

Moreover, one must also bear in mind the limited value and relevance of theoretical principles for actual practice, even in an age notorious for its critical ferocity and its disputes over the rules of literary art and the merits of standard authors. In Renaissance poetry and painting alike, there is often a notable discrepancy between practice and theory. This was more or less inevitable in an age still committed to the principle of authority in the arts and sciences no less than in church and state. Since the major authorities for *studia humaniora* were the ancients themselves, they would necessarily be invoked in controversies over contemporary trends in literature or painting. The rhetorical advantages they afforded in literary or artistic disputations were not to be lightly dismissed, and contestants on both sides of an issue frequently appealed to classical authority, pitting one writer against another or the same writer against himself. One could defend apparent breaches of art as strokes of genius, or justify them by the example of major poets. One could counter appeals to Aristotle or Cicero with allusions to Plato or Seneca. One could rebut an opponent's inferences from Aristotle's *Poetics* by inferences drawn from Aristotle's *Rhetoric* or *Ethics* or *Politics*. One could accept an opponent's authorities as valid, but argue that he had mistranslated them or misconstrued their meaning. Although some of these critics boldly asserted their independence of classical precept and example, they frequently based this argument on the example of the ancients themselves—the liberty exercised by earlier poets and the priority of free invention over the rules of art.

Criticism of the arts of design in the late sixteenth and seventeenth centuries is often heavily indebted to Aristotelian and Horatian poetics, and apologists for very different styles sometimes invoke the same authorities and appeal to the same theoretical principles. If one is to convince an opponent, one must, after all, find a common ground for debate. As recent art historians have observed, the theories of the visual arts during this pe-

21

riod rarely explain or elucidate the development of contemporary styles; and the terms and principles utilized to defend or deride these styles are sometimes transferred intact from classical criticism. This anachronistic vocabulary and methodology are partly responsible for the embarrassment that the art historian usually experiences in attempting to define the developments of late Renaissance style and to fix the meaning of concepts such as "mannerist" and "baroque." The literary historian must reckon with an analogous discrepancy between theory and practice, though usually in a lesser degree; but the difficulties of defining "mannerist" and "baroque" styles in literature are more formidable than in art history.

Since an appeal to the testimony of authors was traditionally a form of inartificial proof, its validity depended largely on the reliability of the author. Although it possessed less persuasive force than logical demonstration through syllogisms or enthymemes, there nevertheless remained one form of testimony that had been traditionally accepted as superior to human reason. This was the divine testimony of the Scriptures as interpreted by the inner illumination of the Spirit which had originally inspired them (if one were John Milton) or by the traditions of the Church (if one were a Catholic). In the context of the Reformation and Counter-Reformation, the literary theorist or the critic of the visual arts could circumvent the authority of classical antiquity by appealing to a higher authority. Divine poetry or sacred art might legitimately follow patterns established by Scripture or by ecclesiastical tradition, even if this meant violating classical norms. Milton could argue, in fact, that the arts of sacred tradition were anterior and superior to those of the Greeks, and that the latter had imitated the sacred arts badly. As a rule, however, Reformation and Counter-Reformation writers achieved a compromise between classical and sacred tradition, retaining the basic principles of classical rhetoric and poetics but emphasizing sacred subjects and ends.

This is also true, in large part, of Milton's major poetry—classical in form and technique, but divine in its subject matter and its orientation, in its material and final causes. His poetic theory is essentially the Renaissance conception of "ideal" imitation—the delineation of abstract concepts in and through sensuous forms that have themselves been abstracted from nature and idealized by art. The visible is a medium for realizing the invisible, and the particular a means of ascent to the universal idea. In form, his major work is not only neoclassical but in some respects archaic. In *Samson Agonistes* he goes behind the prevailing Senecan tradition in Renaissance neoclassical tragedy to the structural pattern of Greek drama. In *Paradise Lost* he retains the essentially tragic emphasis that he had found in the *Iliad* and, to a certain extent, in its Virgilian ectype and the epics of Statius and Lucan. In both of these works the boundaries between the heroic and the tragic are more fluid and less sharply marked than they had been for many Renaissance poets and theorists.[2]

In this respect he is closer, not only to the actual practice of Greek epic and tragic poets (who had sometimes treated the same heroes and indeed the same incidents), but also to the discussion of epic and tragedy in Aristotle's *Poetics*. For Aristotle, epic and tragedy imitated the actions of the same class of persons (*spoudaioi*) and sometimes the same events; they differed primarily in their mode of imitation, in their length, and in the opportunity they afforded for the improbable ("the chief factor in the marvellous"). They were comparable in their subspecies (simple, complex, pathetic, ethical) and in the structure of their plots. He compares Homer to Sophocles as an imitator of "good men" and emphasizes the close relationship between the Homeric epics and "our tragedies." In the "serious style" Homer is "the poet of poets, standing alone not only through the literary excellence, but also through the dramatic character of his imitations."[3] In selecting as

2. For Seneca as a model for tragedy in Italian poetic theory and practice, see Bernard Weinberg, *A History of Literary Criticism in the Italian Renaissance* (2 vols.; Chicago, 1961), I, 103, II, 922; Rosario P. Armato, "The Play Is the Thing: A Study of Giraldi's *Orbecche* and Its Senecan Antecedents," in Rosario P. Armato and John M. Spalek (eds.), *Medieval Epic to the "Epic Theater" of Brecht* (Los Angeles, 1968), 57–83. For Trissino's introducing the tragic chorus after the Greek fashion and for critical comments on his *Sofonisba* as an exemplar of the "idea" of tragedy, see Weinberg, *History of Literary Criticism*, II, 667–68; *Enciclopedia Italiana*, s.v. "Trissino."

3. *Aristotle on the Art of Poetry*, trans. Ingram Bywater (Oxford, 1945), 27, 30–31, 83, and *passim*.

a "Subject for Heroic Song" an argument that he himself de-scribes as tragic and that he had once seriously considered as a subject for a tragedy, Milton broke with the traditional Renais-sance conception of what the subject for a heroic poem ought to be. Although a few Renaissance poets and theorists held a similar opinion of the relationship between epic and tragedy and sanc-tioned tragic arguments in heroic poetry, this was, on the whole, a minority view. Many of the early readers of his poem would be baffled or dismayed by this apparent breach of epic decorum.

In choosing a tragic subject, Milton disregarded the preferences of most Renaissance theorists and poets, remaining faithful to an older heroic tradition and to more venerable authorities—to Aris-totle's doctrines concerning the relationship between epic and tragedy and to the tragic subject matter of many of the major epics of classical antiquity. In its consequences for the human race, Adam's fall is more tragic (and ultimately more felicitous) than the fall of Troy and the fate of Troy's principal champion. His revolt and disobedience are more disastrous than the civil wars described by Lucan and Statius and Virgil. His "breach Disloyal" is more catastrophic than the breach between Achilles and Agamemnon; the divine anger and judgment it provokes are more fatal than the wrath of Achilles and Turnus, or Juno and Neptune. The "destroy-ing wrath" of Achilles, which consigned so many souls of heroes to Hades and left their bodies a prey to beasts and fowls of rapine, is less tragic than Adam's sin and the divine wrath that condemned an entire race to Hell and exposed the whole universe to the rav-ages of more repulsive scavengers, Sin and Death.

Older than the epics of Homer (in the opinion of Milton and his contemporaries, though not of modern scholars) was another tragic epic—a tragedy of suffering with a final reversal and a happy ending. The Book of Job, alternatively classified as a trag-edy or as a heroic poem, was frequently regarded as coeval with Moses or even earlier. It was, accordingly, the earliest extant heroic poem. Moreover, it possessed canonical authority; it was divinely inspired or actually dictated by the Holy Spirit. Milton once con-sidered it as a model for a "brief epic," and scholars have demon-strated its significance for the themes and genre of *Paradise Re-*

gained and its possible influence on *Samson Agonistes*. Like the protagonists of both of these poems, Job is a suffering hero whose faith and patience are being providentially tested for divine ends that he himself does not know. Like the Christ of *Paradise Regained*, who is being schooled in humiliation and suffering in preparation for his ministry and his Passion, he is an exemplar of the "better fortitude" of patience and heroic martyrdom. Except for the brief narratives at the beginning and end of the book, the presentation, or mode of imitation, is predominantly dramatic, consisting largely of dialogue and debate. The dramatic situation is resolved (as in *Samson Agonistes* and in Milton's draft for a drama on Phineas) by a *deus ex machina*, the direct intervention of God. The action eschews a martial argument and centers instead on spiritual combat—the ordeal of temptation, with divine permission, by Satanic agency. The entire work is essentially a theodicy, a vindication of the justice and inscrutability of divine providence.[4]

Many of the themes and motifs developed in the Book of Job recur in *Paradise Lost*—in this case, however, the temptation ordeal results in the hero's defeat. In contrast to Job and the Christ of *Paradise Regained* and the fallen but regenerate protagonist of *Samson Agonistes*, Adam manifestly fails his test. He is an exemplar not of faith or patience or tried obedience but of the frailty of human nature even in its original perfection. As such he serves as an argument *a majori* to remind the poet's audience of the frailty of their own condition, further weakened by Adam's fall, and the necessity of complete reliance on divine grace.

In the Book of Job, the tragic and the heroic are not sharply differentiated, nor are they always clearly distinguished in Greek epic and tragedy. Milton's preference for the type of heroism that generations of commentators had encountered in this work—the fortitude of patience—and that other writers had celebrated in the agonies of the saints and martyrs and in the Passion of Christ

4. For discussion of the Book of Job as heroic poem or as tragedy, see Charles W. Jones, "Milton's 'Brief Epic,'" *Studies in Philology*, XLIV (1947), 209–27; Barbara Kiefer Lewalski, *Milton's Brief Epic: The Genre, Meaning, and Art of "Paradise Regained"* (Providence, 1966).

would tend to preclude a sharp distinction between the two. The virtue of patience and the ideal of the suffering servant would tend to bring heroic poetry close to the pattern of the tragedy of suffering. In a victorious trial the sufferings of the hero would have tragic overtones; in an unsuccessful trial his ordeal would be tragic in a different sense.

The hero of Milton's tragedy is ultimately triumphant both in moral combat and in a more conventionally heroic act of violence against his adversaries; the hero of Milton's principal heroic poem egregiously fails. The one is an exemplar of faith; the other, of breach of faith. Aside from length, mode of imitation (dramatic and narrative, by Aristotle's definition; dramatic and "mixed," in Plato's nomenclature), and epic or dramatic conventions, the chief differentiae between Milton's heroic poem and his tragedy are emotional. Pity and fear, the tragic passions involved in both, are accentuated in the drama but are mitigated and more subdued in the epic. We are all too aware throughout of Samson's blindness and of an inner torment even more painful than the loss of sight; Adam, on the other hand, suffers pangs of remorse but is exempt from physical agony. Passionate outbursts, lamentations, and complaints and emotion-charged personal encounters dominate the play; in the epic the complaints and laments and invectives are milder and far less prominent in proportion to the total length of the work.

Adam's act brings death into the world and "all our woe," but his actual death lies in the future and outside the limits of the main action. The harshness of exile has been mitigated by consolation and promises of future restoration. The "natural tears" he sheds at his expulsion are promptly dried. Although Death himself is a dramatis persona in the action and although Michael's visionary tableaux include scenes of violent death, the protagonists of the poem are temporarily spared. The emotional contrast between the catastrophe of *Paradise Lost* and that of *Samson Agonistes* and between the delineation and expression of *pathos* in the two poems is impressive.

On the whole, it is the nature and intensity of the poet's deliberate appeals to the passions, rather than the particular virtues or

26

vices of the hero or his ultimate success or failure, that is the most striking difference between Milton's tragic epic and his heroic tragedy. In the same way, his projected tragedy on the Passion—"Christus Patiens"—would have emphasized the affective potentialities of the agony in Gethsemane. His epic on the temptation centers on the ideal of the suffering servant and points forward to the Passion, but it focuses primarily on intellectual combat rather than on passionate emotion or physical and spiritual torment. *Paradise Regained* is essentially an epic of character, just as "Christus Patiens" would have been primarily a tragedy of suffering.

How "REVOLUTIONARY" is Milton's epic theory? The occasional remarks on this subject in his prose are, for the most part, conventional; they are consistent with the critical views of many, though by no means all, of his near-contemporaries. As Renaissance theorists were often divided on fundamental issues, it is sometimes misleading to speak of "*the* Renaissance tradition." Most of Milton's statements on poetics would have seemed valid to a majority or to a substantial minority of sixteenth- or seventeenth-century critics. Although his early plans for dramatic poetry on biblical history contradict Tasso's admonition against scriptural subjects as too sacred for the exercise of poetic license and fictive detail, they are consistent with the views of Castelvetro and other critics and with the actual practice of many patristic and Renaissance poets; moreover, Tasso himself had composed a scriptural epic on the creation of the world.

In emphasizing *dianoia* as well as *mythos* as a source of "passion and admiration," Milton is less revolutionary than he may at first appear. Aristotle's *Poetics* had stressed the kind of incidents that might most effectively arouse the tragic emotions of pity and fear, but he had specifically associated *dianoia* ("thought") with rhetoric. Passion and admiration were traditionally associated with the *genus grande* in rhetoric—or, in the opinion of Demetrius and Tasso, with the grave and magnificent styles, respectively. For Longinus, the two principal sources of the sublime and the effect of admiration had been a "firm grasp of ideas" ("great genius" and "great thoughts") and "vigorous and inspired emotion." Aristotle's *Rhetoric* had emphasized the verbal means of exciting admiration (Book I, Chapter 11; Book III, Chapter 2); and late Renaissance critics had elaborated his doctrines into a theory of the *concetto* ("thought" or "conceit") as a source of marvel.

Finally, the poetics of both Aristotle and Horace had stressed the representation and expression of passion. Just as Milton's reference to the "changes of . . . fortune from without" reflects the traditional Aristotelian conception (and indeed the conventional medieval view) of the tragic plot, his allusion to "the wily subtleties and refluxes of man's thoughts from within" is consistent with classical and Renaissance conceptions of the representation of *dianoia* and *pathos*. In Aristotle's *Poetics*, moreover, the term *pathos* may denote both external and internal action, the tragic incidents themselves and the tragic emotions; in Renaissance criticism, *perturbatio* may refer both to the internal emotion and to the events of the tragic (or indeed the comic) plot. In associating both senses of this word, Milton is following Renaissance critical tradition. What appears at first glance to be an innovation on Aristotle's conception of the tragic *peripeteia* turns out to be no innovation at all—merely a logical association between two different senses of *pathos* or *perturbatio*, or passion.

The ideas expressed in the literary apologies prefixed to *Paradise Lost* and *Samson Agonistes* are also traditional, though they represent a minority view. In both poems Milton returns to the practice of the ancients themselves, and in both prefaces he defends his violation of contemporary conventions by appealing, legitimately, to classical example. In both instances he represents himself as a partisan of the ancients against the moderns; but he also reinforces his argument by citing other moderns (chiefly Italian) who had similarly endeavored to restore classical practice. In both cases he is fully aware that he is pleading as a defendant, and (as in his *Defensio Pro Se*) his apology is sometimes truculent. Rhyme is the "Invention of a barbarous Age" rather than a "necessary Adjunct or true Ornament of Poem or good Verse," especially in longer works. Although some "famous modern Poets" have employed it, they were carried away by custom and wrote the

28

worse for the handicap of rhyme. Far from being a "defect" (though "vulgar Readers" may regard it as such), Milton's neglect of rhyme is an act of heroic deliverance—"an example set, the first in *English*, of ancient liberty recover'd to Heroic Poem from the troublesome and modern bondage of Riming."

In attributing the invention of rhyme to medieval barbarism, Milton is exploiting the same tendentious argument that Renaissance humanists had directed against Scholasticism, Reformation theologians against the allegorical interpretation of Scripture, neoclassical theorists against the romance and the conventions of popular drama, and art critics against "Gothic" and Byzantine styles. His appeal to modern examples is, on the whole, less just than his citation of classical precedent. The Italian "Poets of prime note" who had rejected rhyme in *longer* narrative poems were comparatively few, and the Spanish fewer. Unrhymed verse was not uncommon in Italian translations of classical poetry, and it was common in Italian tragedy (except for lyrics and choral odes) as in "our best *English* Tragedies." Nevertheless, in the majority of Italian heroic poems—epics as well as romances—ottava rima remained the conventional verse medium. Neither Trissino's heroic poem on the defeat of the Goths nor Tasso's epic on the creation of the world (both in blank verse) could compare in popularity, influence, and literary merit with the latter's *Gerusalemme Liberata* or with the epic romances of Boiardo and Ariosto.

In defending his tragedy in "the ancient manner, much different from what among us passes for best," Milton again strengthens his valid appeal to classical precedent with a more dubious appeal to Italian example. The Chorus is "here introduc'd after the Greek manner, not ancient only but modern, and still in use among the *Italians*. In the modeling . . . of this Poem, with good reason, the Ancients and *Italians* are rather follow'd, as of much more authority and fame." In actuality, the Greek model was comparatively rare in Italian tragedy. A few dramatists had emulated Trissino in imitating the Greek rather than the Latin form of tragedy, but the majority had preferred the Senecan model.

In both of these cases Milton justifies an apparent breach of poetic conventions by citing the example of the ancients. In the opening lines of the ninth book of his epic, he defends another, and more significant, violation of epic conventions—the rejection of a martial argument—on the grounds of heroic decorum. Battles, games, tournaments, feasts—these conventions of classical epic or chivalric romance are merely

> The skill of Artifice or Office mean,
> Not that which justly gives Heroic name
> To Person or to Poem. (IX, 39–41)

Milton was not, in fact, the first epic poet to "indite" a subject other than "Warrs, hitherto the onely Argument/Heroic deem'd"—just as he was not the first to describe Christ's temptation, despite his assertion in *Paradise Regained* that these "deeds/ Above Heroic" have been left "unrecorded . . . through many an Age." It would be churlish, however, to deny him the traditional license of the poet or orator to heighten an assertion by hyperbole; his statement may be slightly exaggerated, but it is nevertheless true of both the classical and the Renaissance epic traditions, taken as a whole.

In this respect his poem is, in fact, poetically "heterodox," though he himself would probably have regarded it as a return to literary orthodoxy—a reorientation of the heroic poem toward the spiritual combat of the temptation ordeal and toward the true norms of heroic virtue, heroic patterns manifested in the "divine epic" of the Book of Job and in the life and passion of the Second Adam.

He does not defend another apparent breach of Renaissance poetic "orthodoxy" (if one may apply such a term to a tradition all too multifarious and at times contradictory)—the choice of a tragic argument for a heroic poem—nor did he need to. The example of the tragic epics of antiquity and the authority of the *Poetics* of Aristotle would have been sufficient justification. Like his apparent innovations in verse and dramatic structure, his tragic subject appears to be consistent with classical example, though not with the theory and practice of the majority of the moderns.

In his earlier treatises Milton had censured his own contemporaries for their neglect of poetic decorum. Having learned the laws of the genres and "what decorum is, which is the grand master-

30

piece to observe," the pupils of his ideal academy would, as he states in *Of Education*, "soon perceive what despicable creatures our common rhymers and play-writers be, and . . . what religious, what glorious and magnificent use might be made of poetry, both in divine and human things." In *The Reason of Church-Government* he deplores the "corruption and bane" that "our youth and gentry . . . suck in daily from the writings and interludes of libidinous and ignorant poetasters, who, having scarce ever heard of that which is the main consistence of a true poem, the choice of such persons as they ought to introduce, and what is moral and decent to each one, do for the most part lap up vicious principles in sweet pills to be swallowed down, and make the taste of virtuous documents harsh and sour."[5] It is essentially on the grounds of decorum that he condemns the martial epic; its conventional themes fall short of true heroic elevation, of the true decorum of a hero or heroic poem. Again, it is on the basis of decorum that the Christ of *Paradise Regained* censures the poets of Greece; they have extolled their own vices and those of their gods, and for the true decorum of praise he must turn to the songs of Zion, "Where God is prais'd aright, and Godlike men,/ The Holiest of Holies, and his Saints" (IV, 348–49).

The complaint that the celebrated virtues of the Gentiles were vices is an old one, and the accusation that Homer "had written indecent things of the gods" is still older. Milton alludes to it in his *Apology for Smectymnuus*, in which he deplores as "the same fault of the poet" of "lofty fables and romances" the violation of a knight's oath to defend a woman's chastity. He censures those lyric poets who had spoken "unworthy things of themselves or unchaste of those names which before they had extolled." He insists that the poet who hopes to write well "in laudable things" ought himself to be a "composition and pattern of the best and honorablest things." He should not presume to "sing high praises of heroic men or famous cities" unless he possessed in himself "the experience and the practice of all that which is praiseworthy."[6]

5. John Milton, *Of Education* and *The Reason of Church-Government*, both in *Complete Poems and Major Prose*, 637, 670.
6. Milton, *An Apology for Smectymnuus*, in *ibid.*, 693–94.

Milton diverges significantly from the classical and Renaissance epic tradition in the rejection of a martial argument in favor of spiritual combat; the correlative substitution of rhetorical *suasoriae* and dialectics for the clash of arms; the choice of a protagonist notable for his weakness rather than his strength; the conversion of the principal "machining persons" into contrasting images of true and false heroism; and the idealization of a heroism that aspires to servitude rather than dominion and voluntarily submits to shame instead of pursuing glory. These points reflect his revaluation of heroic decorum in light of Protestant ethics. What is fitting to fallen or regenerate man or to the first or second Adam is not what a classical poet, ignorant of the Fall of Man and of the need for utter reliance on grace, would have regarded as the appropriate *ethos* of a hero. When Milton spoke of his one literary advantage over "the greatest and choicest wits" of other nations, he was speaking of his religion: "with this over and above of being a Christian." Perceiving more clearly than the ancients the essence of true heroism and the grounds and limitations of human virtue, he might achieve a heroic poem that would be more truly heroic than theirs, soaring above the Aonian mount with the aid not of Calliope, the traditional muse of epic poetry, but of the "muse Chrétienne," Urania.

Milton's poetic "heterodoxies" are few, but they are all the more impressive for his general fidelity to neoclassical epic principles and to epic conventions. They result primarily from his inner transformation of the standard literary genres through the choice of scriptural arguments and a Protestant frame of reference.

Between Milton's early remarks on his literary tastes and ambitions and the composition of his neoclassical epic on the Fall, he appears to have experienced a growing dissatisfaction with the matter and methods of romance epic. In his essay on *Paradise Lost*, Wayne Shumaker emphasizes three contrasts (besides the substitution of blank verse for ottava rima) between Milton's epic and those of Boiardo, Ariosto, and other Italian poets: "the choice of a simple rather than a complex" (*i.e.*, episodic and multiple-stranded) plot; the rejection of magic; and the substitution of other "ruling interests" for "those operative" in Italian epic—

"valor, honor, and romantic love."[7] In *L'Allegro* the poet had delighted in contests of wit or arms in contention for a lady's favor. In *Il Penseroso* he had enjoyed "sage and solemn tunes"

> Of Tourneys and of Trophies hung,
> Of Forests, and enchantments drear,
> Where more is meant than meets the ear. (ll. 118–20)

In *Comus* he had praised the hidden wisdom concealed in the marvelous fictions of "sage Poets"—marvels that occur not only in classical myth but also in Renaissance romance: "Of dire *Chimeras* and enchanted Isles,/ And rifted Rocks whose entrance leads to hell" (ll. 516–17). Such tales are not "vain or fabulous," for "such there be, but unbelief is blind." In *An Apology for Smectymnuus* he had expressed his delight in "those lofty fables and romances, which recount in solemn cantos the deeds of knighthood founded by our victorious kings, and from hence had in renown over all Christendom." In *Areopagitica* he had extolled the "sage and serious poet Spenser" as a better teacher than Scotus or Aquinas.

In *Paradise Lost*, on the other hand, he brands much of the paraphernalia of chivalric epic and romance as low ("mean") or fabulous: the combats of "fabl'd Knights/ In Battels feign'd," "tilting Furniture, emblazon'd Shields," "gorgeous Knights/ At Joust and Tournament." The monsters—and enchanted groves, if not enchanted islands—are consigned appropriately to Hell, the site of disordered fantasy and disordered nature, where nature herself breeds

> Perverse, all monstrous, all prodigious things,
> Abominable, inutterable, and worse
> Than Fables yet have feign'd, or fear conceiv'd,
> *Gorgons* and *Hydras*, and *Chimeras* dire. (II, 625–28)

One must recognize the rhetorical function of Milton's censure of chivalric conventions in Book IX; nevertheless, the contrast with his earlier praise of symbolic tournaments and enchantments is striking. Like his rejection of a martial argument, his preference for a neoclassical plot structure, and his tendency to restrict

7. Wayne Shumaker, "*Paradise Lost* and the Italian Epic Tradition," in Amadeus P. Fiore (ed.), *Th'Upright Heart and Pure* (Pittsburgh, 1967), 87–100.

the functions of allegorical presentation in the interests of veri-similitude and probability (associating the majority of his allegorical figures or incidents with Hell or with infernal agents or allies), his rejection or transformation of chivalric conventions apparently points to a change in his literary tastes and principles. There are analogies between Adam and romantic heroes (and they enable Milton to exploit the *topoi* of woman sovereignty and the idolization of beauty), but they serve to undercut the romantic tradition. There are also analogies between Satan and the Saracen kings or warriors of chivalric romance (Rodomonte, for instance), but these likewise undermine the romantic *ethos*. In considering Milton's relation to the Italian romantic tradition, however, we must recall that many of the principal Italian poets had themselves undercut this tradition—Ariosto by irony, Pulci and Tassoni by burlesque, Tasso by overt moral criticism of the sensual bondage of Tancred and Rinaldo.

2

"SUBJECT FOR HEROIC SONG"

THE CHOICE OF AN EPIC THEME

"LONG CHOOSING, and beginning late," Milton was understandably slow in deciding on the Fall of Man as the subject for his long-projected, and long-delayed, epic poem. His indecision on this point is all the more striking since he had demonstrated an early and continuous interest in this theme as an argument for tragedy. Although other factors must have contributed to his delay— the magnitude of the task, the need to exercise his skills of organization and expression in less ambitious genres, and the pressure of official duties—the importance that Renaissance poetics had attached to the search for an epic argument could have been a significant deterrent. For in selecting his subject matter, the heroic poet was theoretically required to consider not only its fitness to receive the "ideal form" of an epic plot but also its potentialities for delineating an "ideal pattern" of heroic virtue. His choice of theme would be conditioned by critical theories concerning the disposition and "economy" of his fable, and also by the moral or religious principles he intended to convey. In addition to the formal literary possibilities of his theme, he must take into account the opportunities that it might afford him as a vehicle for ethical and political doctrines.

For many of Milton's contemporaries, the choice might in large part be determined by one or more of a wide variety of factors: the poet's own tastes or those of his patron and his prospective audience; the particular ancients or moderns whom he hoped to

imitate or even surpass; his civic or national or ecclesiastical loy-
alties. The authority of his sources would be a further considera-
tion. He would almost inevitably be attracted to a theme that
might enable him to display his powers of invention and expression. The comparative novelty of his theme might afford greater
scope for his own originality and also prove attractive to his readers. In the context of Renaissance theory, however, one of the
most important factors would be the potentialities that a subject
offered for portraying an exemplary hero in an exemplary action.

The principles that actually governed Milton's choice of subject, however, must on the whole remain conjectural. To judge by
the evidence of the Trinity manuscript and Edward Phillips' account of the composition of *Paradise Lost*, Milton had favored this
argument as a subject for tragic drama above all other scriptural or
national themes. This early preference, together with a growing
awareness of its epic potentialities, would have been "sufficient
reason" for his choice. Yet the clearest evidence of its possibilities
as a "Subject for Heroic Song" as he perceived them seems to be
the testimony of the poem itself.[1]

As a STUDENT at Cambridge, Milton was already aspiring to no
middle flight. Eager to exercise his native tongue in "some graver
subject," he announced his future ambitions to "soar/ Above the
wheeling poles," to "look in" at "Heav'n's door," to inspect the
regions of fire and air and sea, and to relate the primeval secrets of
nature and the deeds of ancient heroes and princes. Some three
decades later, at the beginning of his major epic he expressed a still
loftier intent "to soar/ Above th' *Aonian* Mount" of the classical
muses, pursuing "Things unattempted yet in Prose or Rhyme." In
Paradise Regained he invoked a divine muse to bear him "through
height or depth of nature's bounds/ With prosperous wing full
summ'd to tell of deeds/ Above Heroic." Although such flight
images are conventional, they are an index of the pitch of his ambitions. They reveal a rare head for heights—few symptoms of

1. See Edward Phillips, *The Life of Milton*, in *Complete Poems and Major Prose*, ed.
Merritt Y. Hughes (New York, 1957), 1034–35.

acrophobia—and one might easily overlook the misgivings expressed midway in his heroic fable, the fear of falling "from this flying Steed unrein'd" as Bellerophon had fallen.

Despite the magnitude—and altitude—of his poetic schemes, Milton was slow to attempt the major genres. He was a cautious aeronaut, mindful of the hazards of his art. Unlike Icarus, he insisted on testing his artificial wings in lower reaches of the air before committing them to more arduous and more perilous flights. Like Virgil and Vida and Spenser, he exercised his talents in lesser genres before attempting an epic poem. He described himself—correctly—as "long choosing, and beginning late" since "first this Subject for Heroic Song/ Pleas'd me." It had pleased him, in fact, very early. Roughly two decades before he commenced his epic in earnest, he was preparing alternative drafts for a tragedy on this theme; and his early plans had already undergone further revision when, according to his nephew, he actually began an abortive drama on the loss of Paradise. It was considerably later (*ca.* 1658) that he finally developed this theme as a true "Subject for Heroic Song."

In the meantime he had apparently abandoned his ambitions for a national epic. So far as we can ascertain from allusions in his earlier poetry and prose, these had been at best tentative and uncertain. In *Mansus* and *Epitaphium Damonis* he had expressed a preference for several British subjects—King Arthur and the heroes of the Round Table, Brutus' arrival in Britain (a theme analogous to the argument of the *Aeneid*) and others— but he did not allude to them afterward. There is no indication that he had positively committed himself at this time to an epic centered upon Arthur rather than upon Brutus or Brennus or other British heroes, or that these were schemes for the immediate future rather than long-range projects. In his dramatic "jottings," written after his return from Italy, he had cursorily noted the analogy between the exploits of King Alfred the Great and those of Ulysses and recognized the possibilities of Alfred's wars against the Danes as an epic subject. This was merely a suggestion, however, and apparently he never considered it seriously. In *The Reason of Church-Government* he was still undecided as to "what king or knight before the conquest might be chosen in whom to lay the pattern of a Christian hero" and as to what "model" of the epic he should follow; he was still uncertain as to what genre would be best to undertake—epic, dramatic pastoral, tragedy, or lyric. (His plans for tragedies include pastoral drama in addition to one epic subject.) Francis Peck's assertion that Milton had actually planned an "Arthuriad" in imitation of the *Iliad* and an epic on Alfred in imitation of the *Odyssey* cannot be substantiated by the evidence available to us. William Riley Parker's belief that Milton actually began an epic on King Arthur rests on a dubious interpretation of the *Epitaphium Damonis*. As there is no evidence that Milton ever contemplated an epic on Arthur as a project for the immediate future, speculations as to why and when he abandoned this scheme are, it seems, little more than castles in the air.[2]

It is significant, however, that at a time when Milton was considering biblical as well as national themes as subjects for drama, he was nevertheless (to judge by the available evidence) thinking in terms of a national rather than a biblical epic. In his dramatic notes, scriptural themes far outnumber the entries based on English, British, or Scottish history; moreover, all of the subjects that he develops in detail are biblical. At this time he seems to have preferred divine drama to national drama. Nevertheless, despite his expressed admiration for the Book of Job as a "brief model" for the epic, he did not discuss the potentialities of biblical history as subject matter for heroic poetry. His epic ambitions were confined to "our own ancient stories."[3]

In the three major poems of his maturity, Milton exhibited the same preference for scriptural themes that he had demonstrated much earlier in the more detailed dramatic sketches in the Trinity manuscript. The most notable development in his critical thought is that he extended this preference for a "divine" theme to the heroic poem and that biblical subjects displaced British and English

---

2. See Francis Peck, *New Memoirs of the Life and Poetical Works of Mr. John Milton* (London, 1740), 6, 86–87; William Riley Parker, *Milton: A Biography* (2 vols.; Oxford, 1968), I, 186–87.

3. John Milton, *The Reason of Church-Government Urged Against Prelaty*, in *Complete Poems and Major Prose*, 669.

material as epic arguments. The operations of divine providence, which he had once regarded as a promising theme for "glorious and lofty hymns," he now celebrates in epic and tragedy, justifying and extolling the ways of God to men explicitly through choral passages and implicitly through the providential design manifested in the complication and denouement of his epic or dramatic fable.

In his late poems there are further analogies to his earlier poetic ideals, but there are also significant differences of emphasis. Whether his tragedy portrays the "victorious agonies of martyrs and saints" depends on whether the moral and religious traits that Samson exhibits in his heroic *agon* really fit Milton's conception of the saint or the martyr. Irene Samuel has persuasively challenged Samson's right to the title of martyr; and Mason Tung has stressed his want, rather than his demonstration, of the heroic patience that is the habitual exercise of saints.[4] Even though we may find valid grounds for conceding him these magnificent titles—as literally a *witness* to his faith and as a hero specially consecrated and *sanctified* to his predestined mission—we must nonetheless find him an imperfect exemplar of the "better fortitude" of heroic martyrdom and of the ideal sanctity. It is conceivable that, in his later poetry, Milton's keen sense of the "vanity of human merits" made it impossible to portray these ideals in their perfection except in one "perfect Man, by merit call'd" the Son of God. The hero of *Paradise Regained* is the "great mystery of godliness," and his essential "mystery" remains almost as inscrutable at the conclusion of his ordeal as at the beginning. The coincidence of the human and the divine in the person of the Messiah is undefinable, in the victorious *agon* of Milton's epic as in his theological treatise. Satan has encountered a deeper riddle than that of the Sphinx, and it is not surprising that he fails to solve it.

In this later poetry, another motif that Milton had previously

4. See Irene Samuel, "*Samson Agonistes* as Tragedy," in Joseph Anthony Wittreich, Jr. (ed.), *Calm of Mind: Tercentenary Essays on "Paradise Regained" and "Samson Agonistes" in Honor of John S. Diekhoff* (Cleveland and London, 1971), 235–57; Mason Tung, "*Samson Impatiens*: A Reinterpretation of Milton's *Samson Agonistes*," *Texas Studies in Language and Literature*, IX (1967), 475–92.

favored—the "deeds and triumphs of just and pious nations doing valiantly through faith against the enemies of Christ"—has also undergone a sea change. Samson stands alone against the organized might of the Philistine army and the organized polity of the Philistine state; his countrymen have refused to follow his example or have shamelessly betrayed him. The Christ of *Paradise Regained* had once aspired to deliver his people by arms, but had promptly rejected violent means for the more humane and more heavenly instrument of persuasion. This motif receives its fullest and clearest development in Milton's *Defences* and secondarily in scenes of angelic warfare in *Paradise Lost*. In the former instance it had been promptly undercut by political events; the English people had voluntarily abandoned and betrayed the "good old cause." In the latter instance Milton himself undercuts this motif and accentuates its inadequacies. The military exertions of the faithful against "the enemies of Christ" result in a stalemate, and only Christ himself—single-handed, but armed with the Father's might—can terminate the war. The *populus angelicus* is scarcely more successful than the *populus Anglicanus* in defending the cause of God; and God himself must (as in *Samson Agonistes*) intervene dramatically and decisively to "vindicate the glory of his name." It is divine power alone, not the deeds of a just and pious soldiery, that must restore peace in heaven and (*a fortiori*, it seems) in the church militant on earth.

The "general relapses of kingdoms and states from justice and God's true worship" recur as *topoi* in all three of Milton's major poems, but in the arguments of two of these works he has significantly altered this motif. In *Paradise Lost* he has shifted his emphasis from the general relapses of nations (already painfully apparent in the latter days of the English Commonwealth) to the *lapsus Adae*, the general fall of mankind in and through Adam's fall. His tragedy, on the other hand, centers on the recovery of a single individual—a unique hero set apart from his fellows by his divinely appointed mission, his own vows, and his miraculous strength—after his earlier transgression and fall.

As an epic poet, committed to the laws of this genre, Milton knew that he must select an argument that would enable him to delineate the ideal form of heroic virtue and to compose his plot in accordance with the principles of epic structure. Although the subject he eventually chose was a theme that most Renaissance theorists and the majority of his own contemporaries regarded as more appropriate to tragedy than to heroic poetry, it possessed undeniable technical advantages from the viewpoint of literary theory. In the first place, it was universally relevant. Its protagonists were the ancestors of all mankind, and upon its central action depended the weal or woe of their entire posterity. It allowed the poet to present through prospective and retrospective episodes the panorama of human and angelic history and the creation, corruption, and ultimate destruction of the world. Dating from the very beginning of human history, it possessed the nobility of antiquity and permitted the poet a comparatively free exercise of etiological myth or etiological logic; he could depict the genesis of the Satanic *regnum* and Satan's enmity to mankind, the origins of tyranny and martial conquests, and the "originals" of human nature.

It possessed the authority not only of history but of sacred history—the divine testimony of the Scriptures. At the same time, the biblical account was sufficiently brief—and the times, the places, and the persons sufficiently remote or obscure— to allow the poet ample opportunity to invent or feign. He would not, as critics had objected about Lucan, forfeit the title of poet for that of historian. The nature of his subject would permit him to exploit the Christian marvelous (as Tasso had recommended), but it did not possess the drawbacks that Tasso had detected in scriptural themes—that they were too sacred to allow the poet to alter or rearrange the events of biblical history or to introduce his own fictions.

The brevity of scriptural sources allowed Milton to organize the incidents of the plot in accordance with the "complex" model that Aristotle had favored and to achieve the formal structure or "idea" of the epic that Tasso had regarded as primary.[5] Milton was

5. For Tasso's discussion of the relationship between matter and form in an epic poem and the various points to be considered in choosing a subject, see his *Discorsi del poema eroico*, Book II, in *Prose*, ed. Francesco Flora (Milan and Rome, 1935), 339–83. For the poet's concern with verisimilitude and the universal, and for the principles gov-

comparatively free, therefore, to amplify his argument through divine and infernal councils and epic machinery, to introduce prophetic or retrospective episodes, to invent dialogues and soliloquies, to develop his allegories of Sin and Death and the Limbo of Vanity, and to insert detailed accounts of such fictional incidents as the construction of Pandaemonium, Satan's journey through Chaos and his encounters with Uriel and Gabriel, his first temptation of Eve and his metamorphosis *after* (rather than before) his triumphant return to Hell. Milton was likewise at liberty to depict the motives of his characters, to invest their actions with probability and verisimilitude, to portray the inception as well as the conclusion of Satan's enterprise, to elucidate the causal structure of the Fall, to invest his plot with reversals and recognition scenes, and scenes of suffering and passion and final consolation. He could also draw on an extensive body of biblical commentary to lend additional authority and probability to the motives of his characters and the events of his plot. Finally, it would be largely through the structure and organization that he conferred on his subject that he would be able to demonstrate the providential design underlying and comprising the Fall of Man and thereby to justify the ways of God to men.

In selecting the theme of the Fall, Milton was not breaking fresh ground; he was nevertheless building where no other epic poet of major importance had built. The Old English *Genesis A* and *B* were virtually unknown, and whether Milton himself knew of their existence is still a matter of doubt. Masenius' Neo-Latin epic *Sarcotis* could hardly have seemed a formidable rival, even if Milton had chanced to read it. His principal rivals in this subject matter would, in his opinion, have been the dramas of poets like Grotius and Vondel, Andreini and Salandra, rather than heroic poems. Whereas a dramatic poem on Adam's fall would have challenged comparison with the works of other Renaissance poets, an

---

erning the construction of the plot and the delineation of character and thought, see Book III, 384–445. For an English translation of this treatise, see Torquato Tasso, *Discourses on the Heroic Poem*, trans. with notes by Mariella Cavalchini and Irene Samuel (Oxford, 1973).

epic poem on this theme would at most find few and insignificant rivals.

Viewed in terms of the technical requirements of the epic fable, Milton's subject matter possessed a dual advantage. As biblical history, it was firmly based on the authority of divine truth rather than on the untrustworthy foundation of human tradition and legend or on the fables and inventions of the human imagination. At the same time it could be amplified by fictional details in order to give appropriate magnitude and logical and affective structure to the plot. It was matter fit to receive the ideal form of the epic genre—or indeed of Aristotle's tragic plot. Finally, it permitted the poet not only to model his epic (in part at least) on Homeric and Virgilian exemplars but to adapt the classical model for the "diffuse" epic to the theme of spiritual warfare and Satanic temptation that he had admired in the divine epic of Job. Through its emphasis on providence and the justice of God's dealings with man, on the *mirabilia* of created nature, and on the trial of faith and patience, the Book of Job anticipates some of the major themes of all three of Milton's principal poems—*Paradise Lost* as well as *Samson Agonistes* and *Paradise Regained*. It has, accordingly, an important bearing on the ethical intent underlying Milton's choice of subject in his "diffuse" epic, in his "brief epic," and in his tragedy.[6]

IN INVESTING his argument with the grandeur and magnitude expected of the "diffuse" model of the epic, Milton employed the traditional devices of amplification exploited by earlier heroic poets. Although the nucleus of the principal episodes in the latter part of his fable remains the narrative core derived from Genesis— Eve's temptation by the serpent and Adam's temptation by Eve, the sentence of judgment, and man's expulsion from Paradise—he has fleshed out his narrative with conventional epic paraphernalia. Most of these are his own inventions or else motifs that he has

6. See Charles W. Jones, "Milton's 'Brief Epic,'" *Studies in Philology*, XLIV (1947), 209–27; Barbara Kiefer Lewalski, *Milton's Brief Epic: The Genre, Meaning, and Art of "Paradise Regained"* (Providence, 1966).

adapted from earlier poetic and exegetical treatments of this material. They enable him not only to amplify his argument but also to subject it to the formal requirements of the epic plot, to restructure and reorganize his material in accordance with the principles of unity and decorum, verisimilitude and probability.

These devices were the conventional stock-in-trade of the heroic poet. They were as proper to his craft as the top hat and colored scarves and rabbit to the vaudeville magician. They were so familiar, in fact, that they invited parody as readily as serious imitation. Boileau and other burlesque poets would exploit them for mock-heroic purposes; "Scriblerus" (satiric eponym of Pope and Swift) would ridicule them in a "Receipt" to make an epic poem. These devices enabled a writer to magnify a trivial subject as easily as a heroic argument. Some of them, as Barbara Lewalski and Macon Cheek have observed, proved serviceable to Milton in structuring his "brief" epic on the temptation of Christ and the still briefer epyllion on the Gunpowder Plot. In these shorter poems the introduction of an infernal council serves (as in Claudian's *In Rufinum*) to heighten narrative tension as well as to amplify the argument and to denigrate as diabolical an action or a character that the author deplores. Similarly in *Paradise Lost*, as Irene Samuel and other critics have justly emphasized, much of the dynamic force of the narrative action results from Milton's skillful exploitation of his divine and infernal machinery. This enables him to underline the cosmic and universal significance of the story he found in Genesis by depicting it as one battle in the spiritual war between God and Satan, an episode in the dialectical struggle between the forces of truth and falsehood, creation and destruction, a struggle between spiritual polities based respectively on legitimate and tyrannical dominion, order and disorder.[7]

IN STRUCTURING his plot through a judicious organization of biblical history and imaginative invention, Milton endeavored to

7. See Lewalski, *Milton's Brief Epic*; Philip Macon Cheek, "Milton's *In Quintum Novembris*: An Epic Foreshadowing," *Studies in Philology*, LIV (1957), 172–84; Stella Revard, "Milton's Gunpowder Poems and Satan's Conspiracy," *Milton Studies*, IV (1972), 63–77; Irene Samuel, "*Paradise Lost* as Mimesis," in C. A. Patrides (ed.), *Ap-*

represent the causes of the principal action (as Aristotle had advised), to make Adam's transgression appear probable, and to make diverse effects of his fall—the corruption of sin and death, the sentence of judgment, and ultimately his restoration—seem convincing, plausible or inevitable. Moreover, he must make the principal events of his plot appear to be the probable or necessary consequences of reasoning (thought), moral decisions (character), or previous actions of his personae. The apparent implausibilities in the Genesis account placed all the greater burden upon the poet's art. The Fall itself might seem to strain credulity. On the surface, it is perhaps unlikely that a man and woman created in a state of perfection could so easily be misled (the nature of the "trivial object" itself excites the wonder of Satan's legions) or that an omnipotent, omniscient, and benevolent Deity could permit the devastation of his creation. The motives of all the principal agents—the first man and woman, the devil, Father and Son— must be clearly delineated (and delineated, moreover, in a manner consistent with theological tradition and the doctrines of the Reformed faith) in such a way as to make the central action seem logical and convincing. Even though the Fall of Man was an article of religious faith, the poet could not afford simply to demand assent; he must endeavor to persuade and convince by a probable demonstration.[8]

In essaying simultaneously to assert eternal providence and to depict the Fall of Man, Milton boldly committed himself to prov-

---

prouches to "Paradise Lost" (London, 1968), 15–29; see Frank L. Huntley, "Before and After the Fall: Some Miltonic Patterns of Systasis," in *ibid.,* 1–14, on Milton's exploitation of "the pairs, paradoxes, oppositions, and reconciliations of Christian theology" as the basis for the "reconcilable opposites in the characters," plot, and argument of his epic.

8. In Aristotle's opinion, character and thought (*ethos* and *dianoia*) in tragedy are significant primarily as the causes of actions (and consequently of "success or failure") and for the sake of the plot, which is "the end and purpose," the "first essential," and "the life and soul . . . of Tragedy" (*Aristotle on the Art of Poetry*, trans. Ingram Bywater [Oxford, 1945], 36–38). For beginning, middle, and end in a "well-constructed Plot," see 39–40. For probability or necessity in action, character, or thought, see 41–46, 56–57, 65, 67, 83–87, 91–92. For rhetoric and *dianoia* in Milton's poetry, see Harold A. Dickey, "*Samson Agonistes*: The Dramatic Role of Ratiocination" (Ph.D. dissertation, University of Nebraska, 1969); Hiroko Tsuji, "Rhetoric and Truth in Milton's *Paradise*

ing one of the central paradoxes of the Christian tradition. His proof of this paradox, in turn, depended upon still other paradoxes and marvels of the faith—the oxymoron of the *felix culpa* and fortunate fall, the paradox of strength in weakness and exaltation through humiliation, the paradox of king as servant and liberty in servitude, the miracle of the Incarnation and the oxymoron of the *Theanthropos*, or God-Man. These apparent absurdities on the human level and in the eyes of the world are justified on the divine level and in the eyes of God; for the wisdom of the world (as the poet well knew) is folly in the sight of God—and vice versa. The inherent paradoxes in the poem, the diverse ends of its principal characters, the dialectic of good and evil—these are integrated and reconciled in a single providential vision. The plot of *Paradise Lost* is simultaneously the imitation of an action and the imitation of a divine idea; the design of its plot is the image of a providential design. Underlying the logic of the narrative demonstration is the wisdom of a divine decree. As in *Samson Agonistes* and *Paradise Regained*, the principal reversals in the fable occur against the expectation of some (if not all) of the major characters; but in retrospect they appear probable or necessary.

There is no essential contradiction between the demands of the "logical" epic and the "passionate" epic; for the power of epic or tragedy to produce pity or fear or marvel depends in part on the logical development of the plot. In Aristotle's opinion, the incidents arousing pity and fear "have the greatest effect on the mind when they occur unexpectedly and at the same time in consequence of one another; there is more of the marvellous in them then than if they happened of themselves or by mere chance." The tragic reversal must occur "in the probable or necessary sequence of events." The emotional efficacy of the plot depends in part on its probability, on its logical or seemingly logical construction.

Lost," in *Annual Reports of Studies* (Kyoto, 1969), 348–69. For the logical patterns underlying the Fall of Man as Milton has portrayed it, see Leon Howard, "'The Invention' of Milton's Great 'Argument': A Study of the Logic of 'God's Ways to Men,'" *Huntington Library Quarterly*, IX (1945–46), 149–73; Dennis H. Burden, *The Logical Epic: A Study of the Argument of "Paradise Lost"* (London, 1967); George Musacchio, "'Fallible Perfection': The Motivation of the Fall in Reformation Theology and *Paradise Lost*" (Ph.D. dissertation, University of California, Riverside, 1971).

The "passionate" epic is also the "logical" epic, as Burden and Fixler have sensibly recognized.[9]

IN CONSTRUCTING his tragedy, Milton has achieved a balance between narrative and ethical demands (*mythos* and *ethos*), between argumentation (*dianoia*) and passion (*pathos*), and between heroic and tragic values. Although his argument centers on a moral crisis rather than on the ordeal of arms, he develops it through the narrative devices conventionally associated with the martial epic—councils of war, enterprises of revenge and conquest, the contrasting strategies and tactics of warring kingdoms—and frequently through martial imagery. Nevertheless, the kingdoms are spiritual dominions; the warriors themselves are spirits ("ghostly" foes); and the battleground where they must finally contend is the human heart.

By thus retaining the conventional motifs of the military epic but applying them to an argument based on spiritual struggle, Milton both follows and alters epic decorum. The essential *locus* of a spiritual war must be within, not without, the spirit; and Milton's cosmic battlefield progressively narrows to the soul—the center of man in the center of Paradise in the center of the cosmos. The limitations of Satanic force become progressively apparent; the world conqueror must proceed by craft rather than strength. The strength of the epic protagonist resides in his own free will; it is moral rather than physical fortitude, and the result of the epic action is to demonstrate his frailty rather than his might (in contrast to the majority of epic heroes). The dynamic force of the plot lies in the voluntary actions of the three principal heroic images—Satan, Christ, and Adam—and each of them decisively alters the fate of the world by his act.

Adam loses world dominion, and his loss constitutes the nominal argument of the epic and the major reversal in the plot. Satan conquers the world, but is robbed of the possession of Paradise and the fruition of heroic glory. Until his triumphant return to his

9. *Aristotle on the Art of Poetry*, trans. Bywater, 45, 46; Burden, *The Logical Epic*; Michael Fixler, "Milton's Passionate Epic," *Milton Studies*, I (1969), 167–92.

47

capital, his exploits follow the conventional pattern of the successful imperialist, the heroic conqueror and destroyer. He has conceived and executed his enterprise; and the energy and momentum of the plot depend largely on the poet's skill in converting a "machining person" into a parody of the conventional epic hero. Here again Milton is both observing and undercutting epic decorum—denigrating the values of the heroic age by attributing them to the devil himself. Milton follows and undermines the classical hero in Satan, just as he follows and undercuts the romantic hero in Adam, who sacrifices the lordship of the world and his own life for love. Both are counter-heroes to the Second Adam, who will die for love and will regain and restore the world by renouncing lordship.

Upon these narrative materials, Milton has imposed a formal plot structure containing reversals, recognitions, *pathos* (scenes of suffering intended to arouse or to depict the tragic emotions of pity and fear), and catharsis. For, in the end, the tragic passions are moderated by joy and hope, admiration for the miracle of redemption and ultimate restoration, by inward purification and by the external ministrations of the angel's *consolatio*. Just as the Chorus in *Samson* may depart in "calm of mind, all passion spent," Adam may leave Paradise "greatly in peace of mind," and in hope of his "great expectation," the future Redeemer. As in *Samson*, as in *Lycidas* and the *Epitaphium Damonis*, and as in some of Milton's earlier elegies, the consolatory argument or revelation (itself a form of deliberative oratory) may serve to mitigate pity and fear and grief. The *consolatio* is itself an instrument for moderating the passions and reducing them to "just measure"—a means of catharsis.

3

ARGUMENT MORE HEROIC

EPIC THEME AS DIDACTIC EXEMPLUM

THE INSTRUCTIVE FORCE of a tragic or heroic example hinges, paradoxically, on a fusion of exceptional and representative characteristics, particular and universal attributes. If the emotional impact of an exemplum depends partly on the unusual character of the individual persons and events it portrays, its ethical value resides largely in its generic significance. In his choice of argument and epic protagonists, Milton achieved a compromise between the ethical demand for a universal *moralitas* applicable to the majority of men and the emphasis (traditional in epic literature and criticism) on a heroic individual of extraordinary eminence and virtue.

In the first place, there was the question of the *matter* of virtue or vice, the kind of situation and conditions appropriate for exercising and testing particular virtues. According to both Aristotelian and Christian ethics, virtues and vices alike are habits strengthened by exercise. Conventionally, the matter of temperance is sensuous pleasure, that of patience adversity, that of fortitude danger, that of magnanimity honor and shame. The traditional epic argument of physical combat—"Wars, hitherto the onely Argument/ Heroic deem'd"—may indeed exercise the virtues of fortitude, patience, and temperance, but it does not provide the best or most suitable occasion for trying them, nor does it constitute an adequate test for the higher virtues—for wisdom as a contemplative virtue and for the theological virtues, faith, hope, and charity. All too often, victory falls to the strongest, not

49

to the bravest warrior or the most prudent general. Thus, besides Milton's distaste for a military subject (he is "Not sedulous by Nature to indite/ Warrs"), there is a more cogent reason for rejecting the martial argument: it is not the proper matter of the loftiest, and hence the most heroic, virtues. Primarily the battlefield exercises physical strength and skill at arms; if it demonstrates other qualities, it does so only secondarily. For a trial of truly heroic virtue, the Christian poet must look elsewhere.

In both epics the chief virtue Milton subjects to trial is obedience, and its proper matter is not physical warfare but divine law. For Adam and Eve, the edict against partaking of the forbidden fruit is the "sole pledge of their obedience." The command to obey the Son as the Father's vicegerent and acknowledge him their head tries the obedience of the angels and serves to divide the faithful from the unfaithful. The Father's call for a volunteer to assume man's nature and satisfy divine justice tests the Messiah's obedience to God's will. Similarly, in *Paradise Regained*, the Father's will provides the matter for testing Christ's obedience. Although the poem contains no single edict comparable to the injunction against the fruit of knowledge in the earlier epic, the divine plan for Christ's ministry has already been manifested in the Scriptures; and in rejecting ends and means incompatible with this pattern, the hero proves his obedience. In *Samson Agonistes*, the unfulfilled promise that Samson should deliver Israel from the Philistian yoke provides the matter for his trial of faith.

The other virtues tested in Milton's heroic poetry—wisdom, temperance, charity, patience, magnanimity, fortitude, and the like—also have their proper matter. Samson's patience is tested by adverse fortune and suffering, Abdiel's by shame, Christ's by the tempest and hostile omens in the wilderness. Adam's temperance is tried by Eve, Eve's by the forbidden fruit, Samson's by Dalila, Christ's by the banquet in the wilderness. Samson demonstrates his fortitude in challenging Harapha and voluntarily daring death to destroy his enemies, Christ in undergoing death for the sake of humanity. Satan exhibits a specious fortitude in undertaking the perilous expedition through Chaos, Eve in risking death for the sake of deification, and Adam in electing to die with Eve rather than live without her. Christ displays his magnanimity in rejecting the kingdoms of the world, while Satan and Eve show a spurious magnanimity in the pursuit of vainglory. In *Paradise Lost* Christ manifests his humility by offering to assume man's nature and flesh, in *Paradise Regained* by refusing the "glory and fame" Satan promises him. Milton tests each of these virtues by its proper matter instead of obscuring the moral issue by the argument of war. Even though *Samson Agonistes* culminates in a physical victory over the Philistines, Milton devotes the greater part of the drama to moral conflict; he exhibits Samson's heroic virtues *in animo* rather than on the battlefield. Finally, in *Paradise Regained*, which attempts to demonstrate not only obedience, humility, and patience but the whole complex of heroic virtues, the wide variety of false goods and false evils which Satan proposes provides the matter for exercising an equally wide range of virtues. Milton shows his hero tried and tested "through *all* temptation."

Second, there is the intrinsic worth and magnitude of the subject. Renaissance literary criticism had placed heavy emphasis on the inherent nobility and excellence of the epic argument. Paolo Beni had extolled the argument of the *Gerusalemme Liberata* as superior to those of the Homeric and Virgilian epics. The liberation of Jerusalem is a nobler theme than Achilles' wrath or Odysseus' wanderings or Aeneas' arrival in Italy. In the same way Milton exalts his own argument above those of his classical predecessors. It is "Not less but more Heroic" than the subjects of the *Iliad*, the *Odyssey*, and the *Aeneid*. The particular feature he singles out, in the opening lines of Book IX, for comparison with his own theme is wrath—the ire of gods and heroes. It is Jehovah's anger that is far more to be dreaded: Achilles and Turnus are but men, Neptune and Juno are merely false gods, but Jehovah is all-powerful and his wrath potentially infinite.

Moreover, the "cause" of man's fall, as Milton has already declared, is "Th' infernal Serpent," stirred up "with Envy and Revenge." "Inflam'd with rage," Satan is a far more formidable adversary than these classical gods and heroes. In the context of Book IX, the analogy to Achilles is particularly apt. Like the *Iliad*, the *Avarchide*, and the *Gerusalemme Liberata*, *Paradise Lost* belongs to the "siege tradition," and as the type of the besieged citadel, Paradise itself occupies a position comparable to Troy. The analogy is further strengthened by the parallel between Achilles' pursuit of his foe thrice about Troy's walls and Satan's circling the globe in pursuit of his prey. Both represent much the same type of hero—the destroyer and avenger—and the wrath of both is *oulomenos* ("destroying").

Again, Adam's disobedience resembles Achilles' wrath in the death and destruction it entails; this analogy is implicit in the very proposition of Milton's epic, which echoes the *Iliad*'s emphasis on death. Nevertheless, Achilles' anger dooms numerous Greeks and Trojans to destruction, but Adam's disobedience condemns his whole race. Furthermore, as Milton develops his theme, both divine and infernal anger and man's disobedience itself are transcended by divine love and mercy. "To create is greater than created to destroy," and the motif of destructive wrath is countered by a new creation—the regeneration and renovation of mankind. In this respect too, Milton's subject surpasses the epic arguments of his classical predecessors.

Similarly, Milton's hero excels those of other epics. Adam represents human nature in its original perfection and therefore surpasses the heroes of Homer and Virgil, who, despite their prowess, belong to a fallen and unregenerate humanity. The Christ of *Paradise Regained*, in turn, embodies a still loftier mode of nobility; as perfect God and perfect man, he exhibits the human and divine natures alike at their highest pitch of excellence.

In developing his argument, Milton consciously accentuates particular motifs and episodes which heighten the sense of superiority to classical epic. Homer's heroes conquer a single city; Virgil's hero overcomes a few Italian tribes; Milton's counter-hero conquers a whole world. Where other heroic poems had celebrated battles on land and sea, Milton's describes aerial engagements and warfare in heaven itself. Other heroes had, at most, brought destruction or deliverance to a single nation or a limited society. Satan, however, destroys the whole race of mankind, and Christ delivers "a whole Race lost." Where other poets had celebrated the construction of a city, Milton describes the creation of the universe itself. Although some of these actions are ancillary to his theme, most of them belong to the hexaemeral tradition, and choosing the subject of Adam's disobedience enabled him to develop them.

Again, the fact that it is based not on Gentile fables but on biblical truth lends additional luster to Milton's theme. Neptune and Juno were false deities, and the historicity of the *Iliad*, *Odyssey*, and *Aeneid* was decidedly dubious. Both Homer and Virgil had been accused of distorting historical fact in order to exalt their respective heroes. Romantic epic, in turn, had largely forsaken reality for fairyland. Its characters and events belonged, for the most part, to the realm of fiction rather than fact—the exploits of "fabl'd Knights/ in Battels feign'd"—and even historical figures like Roland and Charlemagne moved among sorceresses and fays and engaged in adventures largely imaginary. Milton's subject, on the contrary, not only represented historical truth but also possessed the additional authority of the word of God. His chief characters were historical persons, their chief action was historical fact, and the agents of his supernatural machinery were no mere myths, but spiritual realities—the God, angels, and devils of Christian belief.

Another factor in Milton's choice of argument is the analogy between the matter of Troy, treated in classical and Renaissance epic, and the biblical material he exploits in his own heroic poems. In the "celestial cycle," as Kirkconnell has termed it, man's fall bears essentially the same analogy to his restoration in Christ that the fall of Troy bears to the foundation of Rome, Britain, and France. But for Troy's destruction, Francion would never have established the kingdom of France ("Ains que bastir les grands murs de Paris"), Brutus would never have founded Troynovant, Aeneas would never have sailed for Italy and laid the political foundations of Rome. The Trojan defeat is thus the precondition of the kingdoms and empires of western Europe and their future glory. If Milton's Adam plays a role comparable to Paris' in uxoriousness and to Hector's in defeat, the Christ of both epics resembles Aeneas, Francion, and Brutus as the founder of a new kingdom, established after long trial and suffering. *Paradise Lost* is, in effect,

Milton's *Iliad*, just as *Paradise Regained* is his equivalent of the *Aeneid*, the *Franciade*, the *Brut*, and his own projected poem celebrating the exploits of British heroes. The Greek conquest of Troy finds its Christian analogue in Satan's conquest of Paradise; similarly, Aeneas' arrival in Italy has its biblical parallel in the Incarnation and the foundation of the Christian church. Moreover, in representing Adam's defeat as a precondition of Christ's victory, Milton does not only reflect the relationship between Trojan defeat and Roman victory as exemplified in the contrast between Homeric and Virgilian epic. He also conforms to the pattern set by Lucan and Daniel. The *Pharsalia* (albeit ironically) treats the Roman civil wars as the precondition of Nero's felicitous reign:

> Still, if Fate could find no other way for the advent of Nero; if an everlasting kingdom costs the gods dear and heaven could not be ruled by its sovran, the Thunderer, before the battle with the fierce Giants,—then we complain no more against the gods: even such crimes and such guilt are not too high a price to pay. Let Pharsalia heap her awful plains with dead; let the shade of the Carthaginian be glutted with carnage; let the last battle be joined at fatal Munda; and though to these be added the famine of Perusia and the horrors of Mutina, the ships overwhelmed near stormy Leucas and the war against slaves hard by the flames of Etna, yet Rome owes much to civil war, because what was done was done for you, Caesar.

Similarly, Daniel treats the Wars of the Roses as the precondition of Elizabeth's reign:

> What furie, o what madnes held thee so,
> Deare *England* (too too prodigall of blood)
> To waste so much, and warre without a foe,
>
> . . . .
>
> Yet now what reason have we to complaine?
> Since hereby came the calme we did inioy;
> The blisse of thee *Eliza*; happie gaine
> For all our losse: when-as no other way
> The heavens could finde, but to unite againe
> The fatall sev'red Families, that they
> Might bring foorth thee: that in thy peace might growe
> That glorie, which few Times could ever showe.

These secular epics have their own *felix culpa* and their own paradox of the fortunate fall; in constructing his epics on the paradox of Paradise lost and regained and on the Adam-Christ parallel, Milton was applying to sacred epic a pattern already conventional in the heroic tradition.[1]

A FURTHER ADVANTAGE of Milton's subjects lay in their suitability for the epic fable as Aristotle and his commentators had conceived it. Theoretically the epic *mythos*, like the tragic plot, involved the change from happiness to misery or vice versa. Man's fall through Adam and redemption through Christ, involving as they did the greatest conceivable transitions from weal to woe and from sorrow to beatitude, were, accordingly, eminently appropriate for the structure of the heroic poem. Similarly, based as they were on the decree of predestination (the central concept of Book III of *Paradise Lost*, the theological foundation of the protevangelium in Book X, and the precondition of Christ's ministry in *Paradise Regained*), the arguments of both epics were especially appropriate vehicles for emphasizing the concept of divine providence and for contrasting the wisdom and power of God with those of man. In this emphasis both poems resemble the Book of Job. Moreover, as man's fallen nature had made true heroic virtue almost impossible apart from spiritual regeneration and had removed all true merit from apparently heroic exploits, Milton's choice of subject enabled him to explore the limits of man's worth and the preconditions of heroic virtue. In contrasting human vice with divine virtue, man's vanity with Christ's merits, the fallen "old man" with the regenerate "new man," both epics achieved a radical reorientation of the heroic tradition around the pivotal doctrines of Protestant theology.[2]

1. Watson Kirkconnell, *The Celestial Cycle: The Theme of Paradise Lost in World Literature with Translations of the Major Analogues* (Toronto, 1952); Pierre de Ronsard, *Oeuvres Complètes*, ed. Gustave Cohen (2 vols.; Paris, 1950), I, 652; Lucan, *The Civil War*, trans. J. D. Duff (London and New York, 1928), 5–7; Samuel Daniel, *The Civil Wars*, ed. Laurence Michel (New Haven, 1958), 71–72.

2. On predestination, compare John Milton, *De Doctrina*, Book I, Chapter 4; see John E. Parish, "Pre-Miltonic Representations of Adam as a Christian," *Rice Institute Pamphlet*, XL (1953), 1–24; C. A. Patrides, "The Protevangelium in Renaissance Theology and *Paradise Lost*," *Studies in English Literature*, III (1963), 19–30; my "Adam and the Prophesied Redeemer (*PL*, XII, 359–623)," *Studies in Philology*, LVI (1959), 214–25.

Milton's subject serves, furthermore, to demonstrate the superiority of "deeds of peace" to the conventional epic argument of "Warrs." Adam's transgression breeds moral strife and discord, and the war in heaven involves both spiritual and corporeal combat. Nevertheless, both battles conclude with the triumph of peace. In the celestial war, the Messiah not only expels the rebels but also restores to heaven its former order and state of calm. In fallen men he achieves, through spiritual regeneration, a similar peace on the moral and psychological plane. Milton thus has an opportunity for comparing war and peace as contrasting modes of heroic action and for demonstrating the excellence of the latter.

Besides these ethical and theological advantages, Milton's subjects possessed other didactic potentialities. By basing the argument of *Paradise Lost* on Genesis—the "beginning" of things—he was able to depict first causes. For Aristotle, the investigation of causes had been a prerequisite of the knowledge of essences; and in the *De Doctrina* and the *Artis Logicae*, Milton retains the Aristotelian fourfold causality—material, formal, efficient, and final. The subject matter of *Paradise Lost*, derived as it is from the hexaemeral tradition, is admirably adapted for presenting *principia* and origins. As Milton develops these potentialities, he portrays the causes and origins of physical and spiritual entities alike—the creation of the world, the origin of species, the beginning of man, the institution of marriage, the establishment of the infernal and celestial kingdoms (the *civitas terrena* and the *civitas Dei*), the genesis of sin, death, and misery, the source of spiritual regeneration, the origin of hypocrisy and lies, the beginning of warfare, the invention of cannon and gunpowder, and discovery of fire, and the invention of the arts. In particular, however, he stresses the causes underlying the creation and corruption of the world and man—the very points on which the Christ of *Paradise Regained* indicts the Greek philosophers for ignorance. In describing the genesis of the visible universe, Milton depicts the four primary causes—material (the elements of Chaos), formal (God's "great Idea"), efficient (the Son as Logos and Demiurge), and final (the glory of God). In the case of Adam and Eve, the efficient and final causes are again the Son as Word and the glory of God (Adam and Eve are destined to produce "a Race of Worshippers" to fill the void left by the rebel angels), but the material causes are the dust from which Adam is molded and the rib from which Eve is formed; the formal cause is the "idea" of a rational being, endowed with moral freedom and capable of "correspond[ing] with Heav'n."[3]

MILTON'S CHOICE of subject enabled him to imitate the Christian pattern of warfare as set forth by Saint Paul, exemplified in the temptation of Job and the ordeals of saints and martyrs, and elaborated in Erasmus' *Enchiridion Militis Christiani*. Whereas the conventional epic had celebrated the characteristic warfare of the world and the flesh, Milton finds his argument in the scriptural conception of spiritual conflict: "For though we walk in the flesh, we do not war after the flesh: (For the weapons of our warfare are not carnal, but mighty through God to the pulling down of strongholds;) Casting down imaginations, and every high thing that exalteth itself against the knowledge of God, and bringing into captivity every thought to the obedience of Christ; And having in a readiness to revenge all disobedience, when your obedience is fulfilled" (II Cor. 10.3–6). "Finally . . . be strong in the Lord, and in the power of his might. Put on the whole armour of God, that ye may be able to stand against the wiles of the devil. For we wrestle not against flesh and blood, but against principalities, against powers, against the rulers of the darkness of this world, against spiritual wickedness in high places. Wherefore

3. Aristotle, *Metaphysica*, trans. W. D. Ross, and *Ethica Nicomachea*, trans. W. D. Ross, both in *The Basic Works of Aristotle*, ed. Richard McKeon (New York, 1941), 691, 712, 1023; compare Milton, *De Doctrina*, Book I, Chapter 7, in *Complete Poems and Major Prose*, ed. Merritt Y. Hughes (New York, 1957); compare Milton, *Artis Logicae*, in *The Works of John Milton* (New York, 1935), XI, 30–31; Aristotle, *Metaphysica*, 693, 713–15; Aristotle, *Physica*, trans. R. P. Hardie and R. K. Gaye, in *The Basic Works of Aristotle*, 240–41. For a study of Milton's doctrine of the efficient cause, see Leon Howard, "'The Invention' of Milton's Great 'Argument': A Study of the Logic of 'God's Ways to Men,'" *Huntington Library Quarterly*, IX (1945–46), 149–73; compare my "'Man's First Disobedience': The Causal Structure of the Fall," *Journal of the History of Ideas*, XXI (1960), 180–97.

take unto you the whole armour of God, that ye may be able to withstand in the evil day, and having done all, to stand" (Eph. 6.10–3).

The "wiles of the devil," the proud "imaginations" whereby Satan exalts himself against the "knowledge of God," the powers and principalities of Hell, the "spiritual wickedness" of the demons of the air, the force and fraud of the "rulers of the darkness of this world"—these are the Christian warrior's spiritual enemies and the antagonists of his moral conflict. By centering his epics on the temptations of Adam and Christ, Milton was able to present both the norm of Christian warfare and the tactics of the spiritual foe. In developing this pattern, however, he also took pains to contrast it with its secular *eidolon*, the warfare of the flesh. The first descriptions of Satan and his forces emphasize their gigantic stature, their number, and their "embodied force." The spectacle of the Parthian armies, which Christ dismisses as "Mere ostentation vain of fleshly arms," likewise stresses the pattern of secular might. The same false ideal reappears in Harapha and his "carnal reliance" on "glorious arms." In contrast, Samson's *fiducia in Deo* literally proves "mighty through God to the pulling down of strongholds."

Erasmus' *Enchiridion* begins with the reminder that "mortal life is nothing but a kind of perpetual warfare—as Job testifies, a soldier both widely experienced and consistently invincible." Thomas à Kempis makes the same point: "As long as we live in the world we may not be fully without temptation. For, as Job saith, The life of man upon earth is a warfare; therefore every man should beware well against his temptations . . . that the ghostly enemy find not time and place to deceive him, which never sleepeth, but walketh about, seeking whome he may devour." Both writers derive their conception of spiritual warfare partly from Saint Paul and partly from the ordeal of Job. For Milton, as for Isidore, the Book of Job was a heroic poem. It developed the temptation motif into the archetype of spiritual warfare between Satan and the human soul. As in the case of Milton's Adam and Christ (and, indeed, Milton's Abdiel), Satan's temptation ultimately proves the heroic virtue of the righteous. All of these ordeals are "good temptations," in which God uses the devil as an agent to try and illustrate the virtues of the elect. The Book of Job thus provides the basic pattern of Christian warfare, and from it Milton derives his heroic treatment of the temptation motif, his basic conception of the role of Satan, and his emphasis on spiritual combat. Job himself, in turn, through his constancy and his unshaken "trust" in God, sets a heroic example of faith and patience, the "better fortitude." These are two of the virtues on which Milton places primary stress in *Samson Agonistes* as well as in *Paradise Lost* and *Paradise Regained*. Finally, through its emphasis on God's controlling providence, inscrutable justice, and "marvellous works," the Book of Job gave definitive statements to what would become the leitmotifs of Milton's epic and tragedy.[4]

Both the *Enchiridion* and the *Imitatio Christi* take the Vulgate text of Job 7.1, "Militia est vita hominis super terram," as the basis of their conception of spiritual warfare. Gregory's *Moralia* interprets this passage in terms of temptation and warfare against evil spirits. An earlier Latin translation, Gregory observes, had referred to human life not as warfare (*militia*) but as temptation (*tentatio*). The two different words bear much the same sense. For what is meant by the word *temptation* except fighting against evil spirits? And what is meant by the word *warfare* except exercising one's powers against enemies? Thus temptation is warfare: although it watches against the deceits of evil spirits, it undoubtedly toils in readiness for battle.

> Hoc in loco translatione veteri nequaquam militia vita hominis, sed tentatio vocatur. Sed si utriusque verbi sensus aspicitur, diversum quidem est quod exterius resonat, sed unum eumdemque concorditer intellectum format. Quid enim nisi pugna contra malignos spiritus, nomine tentationis exprimitur? Et quid appellatione militiae, nisi contra hostes exercitium designatur? Tentatio itaque ipsa militia est, quia dum contra malignorum spirituum insidias vigilat, in bellorum procinctu procul dubio exsudat. Notandum vero, quod haec eadem vita hominis tentationem habere dicitur, sed ipsa

4. *The Enchiridion of Erasmus*, trans. Raymond Himelick (Bloomington, 1963), 38; Thomas à Kempis, *The Imitation of Christ*, trans. Richard Whitford (New York, 1961), 22; on "good temptations," compare Milton, *De Doctrina*, Book I, Chapter 8, in *Complete Poems and Major Prose*.

tentatio esse perhibetur. Sponte quippe a statu conditionis lapsa, et corruptionis suae putredini subdita, dum sibi ex semetipsa molestias gignit, hoc est jam facta quod tolerat. . . . Sed quia cum culpa simul ab origine etiam poena propagatur, inserto infirmitatis vitio nascimur, et quasi nobiscum hostem deducimus, quem cum labore superamus. Ipsa ergo hominis vita tentatio est, cui ex semetipsa nascitur unde perimatur. Quae etsi semper ex virtute succidit, quod ex infirmitate generat, semper tamen ex infirmitate generat, quod ex virtute succidat.

For Gregory, the warfare of human life is temptation; and this state of perpetual spiritual conflict stems primarily from man's fallen condition and original sin.[5]

The warfaring Christian (Erasmus warns) must fight continually against "ironshod hordes of vices," against the "hellishly slippery serpent, the first destroyer of our peace," and against "that ancient and earthy Adam" in himself. Yet the Christian's rewards are far nobler and more honorable than those of the physical warrior. Those who "serve the world not only serve in a foul cause but for miserable pay," for the "wages of sin is death." In the "insane wars man wages against man," the wretched soldiers seek only a "trifling reward"—"Merely that, in the uproar of battlefield or camp, they be lauded by a captain who is only a man and celebrated in some crudely flattering doggerel, or be decked out in a wreath of grass or oak leaves, or carry home a little larger purse than usual." Christians, on the other hand, "are kindled neither by shame nor hope of reward, even though we have as observer of our efforts the One who will pay us off." As prizes God offers them no mere trifles, but "Life, joyful and everlasting": "Heaven is promised to him who fights valiantly; does not the lively courage of a noble spirit kindle at the prospect of such a happy reward, especially when it is presented by that Creator who is no more able to deceive than not to be what He is? . . . The One whose praise is supreme felicity will praise our courage; why do we not seek this felicity even if it costs us our lives?"[6]

In his battle against sin the Christian's chief weapons are prayer

5. Gregory, *Moralia*, in *Patrologia Latina*, LXXV, cols. 805–806.
6. Erasmus, *Enchiridion*, 38–39, 41–42.

and knowledge—the self-knowledge which is essential for all wisdom and that *philosophia Christi* which the world regards as folly: "Whereas every doctrine of man is tinged by some darkness of error, the teaching of Christ is wholly pure and sound. . . . And if you wish to go now to the armory of Paul, a chieftain by no means sluggish, you will find unequivocally that the weapons of our warfare are not material ones, but that, in God, they are mighty in leveling fortifications, foiling stratagems, and reducing every tower erected against the wisdom of God." The end of this warfare is peace, but this is attainable only through incessant battle against sin: "Peace is that ultimate good towards which even the lovers of this world bend all their efforts, but . . . they grasp at a counterfeit kind. Philosophers used falsely to promise peace to the followers of their teachings, but only Christ bestows that which the world is not able to give. There is only one way of arriving at this peace: to make war upon ourselves, to battle fiercely against our own vices."[7]

Milton too stresses the superior rewards of Christian warfare—divine glory as opposed to the plaudits of the world, eternal life as contrasted with temporary honors terminated by death, spiritual peace as opposed to inner confusion. Death is the final reward of the worldly conquerors, and their vain exploits remain confined to the Limbo of Vanity. The Christian warrior, on the other hand, gains paradise and the praise of God himself as his rewards.

Of the various advantages Milton's choice of subject offered him, this was, perhaps, the most significant in terms of the heroic tradition, for, with its emphasis on spiritual warfare and the crisis of temptation, it placed *Paradise Lost* and *Paradise Regained* firmly in the line of descent from the Book of Job. Although the technique of both of Milton's epics is essentially classical, the type of heroism they celebrate and the kind of crisis in which these heroic virtues are tested and exercised conform to the pattern set by the Spirit itself in the first and archetypal heroic poem. Whereas Tasso, Ariosto, and Spenser present temptation primarily in alle-

7. For Erasmus and the *philosophia Christi*, see *ibid.*, 29–30; J. Huizinga, *Erasmus of Rotterdam*, trans. F. Hopman (London, 1952), 109–10; Erasmus, *Enchiridion*, 49, 57, 59.

gorical terms, Milton follows the precedent of Job in depicting spiritual ordeals through literal presentation. The moral crisis represented in those romance-epics is not altogether dissimilar to that displayed in Milton's sacred epics, but there is a fundamental difference between them in type of argument and manner of imitation. As Tasso draws his subject from physical warfare, he is compelled, in large part, to represent spiritual ordeals allegorically— or at least to claim that a spiritual allegory underlies the literal and surface meaning of the persons and events he is describing. Milton, on the other hand, having chosen a subject based on spiritual combat, could imitate the temptation crisis literally, without having to resort to allegorical methods.[8]

As A POEM of origins, *Paradise Lost* also depicts the contrary beginnings and destinies of the Augustinian *civitas Dei* and *civitas terrena*. As Milton develops them, the contrasts between order and disorder, peace and confusion reflect to a certain degree the contrasting etymological significance of Jerusalem and Babylon, as types of the city of God and the city of the world. As the poet himself points out, the latter derives its name from *confusion*; and it is confusion that regularly (or irregularly) characterizes the Satanic realm, its strategy, and its ultimate punishment. In contrast to the order and peace of the heavenly Jerusalem (*visio pacis*), the kingdom of Hell possesses neither the hope nor the potentiality of peace. From the first, Satan realizes that "Peace is despaired," and the council underlines this fact: no "terms of peace" have yet been

8. In stressing Milton's preference for a "literalistic" rather than allegorical presentation of moral conflict and its bearing on his choice of subject, one should not minimize either the symbolic techniques underlying his representational modes or the more patently allegorical elements in *Paradise Lost*. Besides the allegory of Sin and Death, such symbolic details as the Limbo of Vanity, Jehovah's celestial scales, and Satan's final metamorphosis, and the exploitation of biblical symbolism in several features of the angelic war (Michael's sword, the Messiah's chariot, and the like), the relationship between Adam and Eve could be interpreted allegorically as well as literally. According to Erasmus' *Enchiridion*, the reader should keep "in mind that 'woman' is man's sensual part: she is our Eve, through whom that wiliest of serpents lures our passions into deadly pleasures. Paul would have woman subordinate to the husband. . . . Our Eve is fleshly passion, whose eyes were daily lured by that crafty serpent; and when she had been corrupted, she hurried to entice man into sharing evil with her" (39, 75).

given, and "none will be given." Belial's "sentence . . . advising peace" may please his audience, but the real import of his counsel is simply "ignoble ease and peaceful sloth, not peace."

Underlying the political and military conflict of the heavenly and celestial societies of *Paradise Lost* is the more fundamental antithesis between peace and confusion, order and disorder, obedience and disobedience. In macrocosm and microcosm alike—in the soul, in the family, and in the visible and invisible universe— the hierarchical principle dominates; all exhibit the state of divine obedience and the peace of order. Satan's policy is directly antithetical. Where there is peace, he introduces strife; where there is order, he fosters disorder; where there is obedience, he sows disobedience. Where God creates, Satan destroys. Where God brings order out of Chaos, Satan reduces the created order to confusion. Forming a pact with the gods of the abyss to restore the world to its original chaos, he attempts to "confound the race of mankind in one root." Introducing disorder in microcosm and macrocosm alike, he disrupts the "household peace" of Adam and Eve and destroys their internal peace by the conflict of discordant passions, the "siege of contraries." The harmony of the universe broken, beasts prey on one another and on man. Man wages war against man; against the law of nature, man enslaves man. The elements are altered, and the sun afflicts the earth with intolerable "cold and heat." The planets join in "noxious efficacy" and "Synod unbenign." The fixed stars acquire "influence malignant," and the winds "confound Sea, Air, and Shore." Satan's enterprise intends, and achieves, universal confusion—the extension of "Babylon."

But *confusio* is more than the basis of the infernal strategy; it is also the essential quality of the punishment that divine justice inflicts on the infernal commonwealth. Having broken the peace of heaven by the "attack of fighting Seraphim confused," the rebels themselves meet "treble confusion" and "horrid confusion heaped upon confusion." With its hybrid monsters, its extremes of hot and cold, and its flames devoid of the natural property of light, Hell is itself a realm of confusion. The expedition its citizens dispatch to explore their new domain ends up in a "confused march forlorn." And despite its initial success, Satan's attempt to explore and conquer the new world terminates in confusion and ridicule.

The celestial strategy, on the other hand, is one of bringing order out of disorder and harmony out of chaos. To a heaven torn by rebellion the Son restores order and peace. To the fallen soul rent by conflicting passions he restores internal tranquillity. On the warring elements of the abyss he imposes order. By physical creation and spiritual renovation alike, he restores domains of *confusio*—the external realm of Chaos and Satan's spiritual empire within the human soul—to the peace and obedience of the celestial kingdom.

IN SELECTING and developing the subject of the Fall, Milton had recognized the political possibilities of this theme. It provided him with opportunities for portraying the use and abuse of sovereignty, for depicting the origin of true and false kingship, and for criticizing the pretensions of monarchs to divine right as God's vicegerents. As Milton develops it, the matter of Genesis undercuts the code of royalist and aristocrat, king and cavalier.

The ideas of dominion and authority are of central significance for the structure and argument of *Paradise Lost*. The plot hinges on a breach of feudal loyalty and a violation of authority. In disobeying the command of their feudal sovereign, Adam ranks his love for his wife above his duties to his overlord; Eve rates the evidence of her own senses and the testimony and plausible arguments of her tempter above divine testimony. The fall of the angels had similarly resulted from a breach of feudal allegiance and a rejection of authority; Satan's revolt is motivated by envy of the divine vicegerent—"Messiah, who by right of merit reigns." Milton has presented the hierarchical world order of seventeenth-century belief as a feudal order. Physical and metaphysical hierarchies—the scale of beings leading from the lowest elements in the created universe up to the Deity—are a political order. The divine vicegerent can create by fiat, by regal decree; the elements hear his voice and obey. The "laws" of nature are imposed from above by a divine legislator; they are not only physical or metaphysical laws but true edicts. The feudal dependence of the created world on its creator is visually apparent in the golden chain that links it to heaven; the "pendant World" is also a *de*pendent world.

The even temperatures and mild climate of Eden are the product of order; its elements are tempered and moderated by divine government; and its flora and fauna subjected to the mild and easy government of unfallen man. In contrast, the fierce extremes of Chaos and Hell are indicative of the absence of divine order, though they are nevertheless subject to divine sovereignty and supernal control. World order and world disorder form a single political state—a divine kingdom in which the wisest and best of monarchs governs the forces of order and disorder alike, ruling with golden or with iron scepter in the interests of "public safety" and the common good.

Within this framework of universal monarchy, the entire creation, visible and invisible alike, becomes a political system in which rank is as scrupulously observed as at a Byzantine court, in which title is contingent on merit and dominion based on authority delegated by the sovereign. In this context, moral and religious virtues acquire political overtones. Obedience and disobedience appear as fealty and breach of allegiance; and divine worship as a form of feudal homage. As described in Book V, the angelic nobility—"Progeny of Light,/ Thrones, Dominations, Princedoms, Virtues, Powers"—hold their "happy state" on the condition of obedience. Adam and Eve possess the entire earth as their fief, but on the condition of feudal allegiance; except for "one restraint," they are "Lords of the World." Abstention from the forbidden fruit is

> The only sign of our obedience left
> Among so many signs of power and rule
> Conferr'd upon us, and Dominion giv'n
> Over all other Creatures.   (IV, 428–31)

As Satan himself perceives, this is a sign of fealty, a token of feudal homage and submission: "The proof of thir obedience and thir faith."

Like the hierarchical order in the cosmos, the hierarchy of faculties within the microcosm and the order within the first

human society—the family—inevitably acquire political significance. Adam loses the "true filial freedom" which is the base of
"true authority in men" and forfeits his world dominion by allow-
ing passion to dominate reason and yielding to the persuasions of
his wife. Raphael had, in Book VIII, warned him against "subjection" to his wife and against the tyranny of passion over judgment; and his divine judge reminds him that her beauty should
"attract/ Thy Love, not thy Subjection." "Effeminately vanquish't,"
like Samson and Solomon and many heroes of epic and romance,
Adam is a victim of that "gynaecocracy" which Milton had de-
plored in his earlier writings. Woman sovereignty had been a re-
current theme in the erotic literature of the Middle Ages and the
Renaissance, but Milton was especially interested in its political
implications, either as government by women or as the influence
of wives or mistresses on the policies of kings. This theme appears
in his Commonplace Book, in his plan for a tragedy "Solomon
Gynaecocratumenos," and in "Puritan" criticism of Henrietta
Maria and Charles I. Adam falls through the same weakness that,
in Milton's opinion, had caused the ruin of kings and kingdoms.
Belial was no stranger in courts and palaces.

IN REJECTING the conventional epic subject matter—warfare—
Milton significantly shifted the traditional social and political orientation of the heroic poem. With certain notable exceptions, this
had been for the most part an aristocratic genre, glorifying the
exploits of a military elite and the values of an aristocratic and
courtly society. Horace had advised the heroic poet to portray the
deeds of kings and captains, "res gestae regum ducumque et tristia
bella." Tasso had endeavored to portray the idea of a perfect cavalier, and Spenser to fashion a gentleman. To exhibit the pattern of
a Christian hero, Milton himself had originally looked to British
history, ransacking the pages of the chroniclers for some king or
knight before the Norman Conquest, who might serve as a heroic
exemplar. In Renaissance Italy, writers of chivalric epic or romance had sought patronage at the courts of Ferrara or Urbino,
Milan or Florence or Naples, or even as far afield as the royal court
of France. As a mirror for princes, the epic had portrayed the vir-

tues of a good governor or valiant warrior. As a vehicle for Reformation and Counter-Reformation propaganda, it had exhorted monarchs and noblemen to undertake new crusades and holy wars on behalf of the faith. As an instrument of demonstrative rhetoric, it had eulogized the merits of potential patrons or amplified the exploits of their ancestors. Like the *piano nobile* in some Renaissance palace or the "Monument of merit" celebrating the first world conquest, it was an architecture of encomium, designed for flattery on a grand scale and in the grand style.

The martial epic had inevitably demanded a martial hero; its principal characters had been monarchs and warlords. When Milton renounced physical combat for spiritual struggle, he altered the social and political status of the epic protagonist. The captains and the kings depart. The epic person of *Paradise Lost* is not the founder of a royal dynasty or the head of a princely house but the progenitor of all sorts and conditions of men. In contrast to the peers and monarchs among his posterity, he rules in a natural setting rather than in artificial state. A "Head" of mankind, he exercises his captaincy not in military actions on the battlefield but in the peace and quiet of the domestic scene, governing his wife and commanding the animal and vegetable kingdoms. A world sovereign, he performs his duties primarily in cultivating his own garden. This is *essential* kingship, unadorned and "naked Majestie." The first "Lord" of the earth is invested with "native Honour"—unlike the artificial honor and native *dis*honor of his descendants. He does not require the accidents and superficial trappings of lordship, for he possesses the actual substance: "in himself was all his state." Instead of the military elite of a fallen and artificial social order, the "violent Lords" whose dominion reflected the inner servitude consequent to the Fall, Milton portrays the "natural man" in his original innocence—and subsequently in his fallen condition. Instead of the conflict of secular kingdoms, he depicts a more basic rivalry between older and more enduring spiritual empires—the kingdoms of God and Satan, locked in perpetual struggle for dominion over the soul. For the duels of fabulous knights he substitutes a moral ordeal, the spiritual combat of Everyman.

The protagonist of *Paradise Lost* is a universal hero rather than a class-hero, a representative of the entire *humanum genus* rather than an idealized exemplar of a military and feudal elite. The common ancestor of all men, he undercuts the glorification of heroic genealogy conventional in classical and Renaissance epic. Claims to nobility and dominion on the basis of ancestral birthright may be valid for the Son of God, but not for the sons of Adam, who inherit depravity rather than gentility from the founder of their line. Pride in noble ancestry and hereditary claims ultimately lead back to a rebellious feudal vassal under attainder of treason, a "Lord" who had lost his fief and bequeathed his disgrace to his posterity. In contrast to the descendants of Virgil's epic protagonist and the posterity of Ruggiero and Rinaldo and Artegall, Adam's seed have no cause for glorying in the exploits of their ancestor. Instead of dominion and nobility, he has transmitted bondage and a corrupted blood to his descendants.

All classes of human society, moreover, were equally involved in their common ancestor's fall, sharing the same inherited honor and dishonor. Having forfeited their claims to lordship by birthright, kings and thralls were equally born to moral slavery under the tyranny of Sin and Death, and must seek true nobility by "ingrafting" in another family tree, the stock of another Adam. For peers and peasants alike, "verray gentillesse"—the *nobilitas Christiana*—was contingent on divine grace. "Lords of the World," the epic protagonists of *Paradise Lost* nevertheless transcend distinctions of class.

4

RHETORIC AND POETICS IN THE
PREFACE TO *SAMSON AGONISTES*

OBLIQUELY INTRODUCED in his preface to *Samson Agonistes* in order to support another point—the moral utility of tragedy—Milton's brief allusion to catharsis has proved, on a smaller scale, almost as controversial as Aristotle's own remarks on the subject. Unwittingly Milton plunged his twentieth-century readers into the midst of a sixteenth-century conflict. In modern scholarship on his preface we may recognize yet another skirmish in that Cinquecento battle of the books—the war of commentaries fought over the text of the *Poetics*, uneven but fiercely disputed terrain.

Frequently translated, frequently reprinted, and still more frequently annotated, Aristotle's treatise had engaged not only the foremost Italian critics but also scholars in northern Europe. To the elucidation of his text they had brought the exegetical and philological methods acquired from humanistic or Scholastic disciplines, literary concepts inherited from intensive rhetorical training and the study of Horace and Terence, and a predisposition, unacknowledged and perhaps unconscious, to interpret the "new" and relatively unfamiliar Aristotelian principles in terms of "older," more familiar patterns already established in late medieval

Previously published, in slightly different form, as "'Passions Well Imitated': Rhetoric and Poetics in the Preface to *Samson Agonistes*," in Joseph Anthony Wittreich, Jr. (ed.), *Calm of Mind: Tercentenary Essays on "Paradise Regained" and "Samson Agonistes" in Honor of John S. Diekhoff*, published by The Press of Case Western Reserve University (Cleveland and London, 1971), 175–207. Used with permission.

and early Renaissance theory. The result, as Bernard Weinberg has cogently argued, was "one of the strangest misunderstandings of a basic text in the history of ideas, and the formation of that very curious complex of notions which we call the neoclassical doctrine." [1]

In retrospect, this controversy may seem mere windy disputation, more productive of words than of matter; but, on the whole, it was by no means barren. Critical disputes over Aristotle's text remolded literary criticism and decisively influenced the theory of painting, sculpture, and music. Serving to define problems (even if it did not provide definitive answers to them), formulating issues (even if it did not satisfactorily resolve them), this controversy left its imprint not only on epic and drama but also on the visual arts.

It is against this background that Milton's scattered remarks on poetics and all of his major poetry must be placed. The *Poetics* Milton quotes is, in a sense, a Cinquecento document; to understand what it meant to him, one must approach it through Italian commentators—Tasso, Mazzoni, and their contemporaries—rather than through late Victorian and twentieth-century explicators. In seeking the Aristotle Milton knew, one must in large part divest oneself of interpretations derived from recent Aristotelian scholarship and turn instead to the less accurate but perhaps more relevant observations of Renaissance scholars. One must endeavor to visualize the *Poetics* as it appeared to Castelvetro, Minturno, and Piccolomini rather than to Butcher and Bywater.

The conflicts of these Cinquecento and Seicento critics are still relevant for the Miltonist. Contemporary studies of Milton's interpretation of the *Poetics* are essentially a recapitulation of the earlier Renaissance debate. They have, moreover, inherited the ambiguities of this controversy along with its issues. If students of the preface are still undecided as to what its author meant to say or how he interpreted Aristotle, it is partly because students of the

1. Bernard Weinberg, "From Aristotle to Pseudo-Aristotle," in Elder Olson (ed.), *Aristotle's "Poetics" and English Literature: A Collection of Critical Essays* (Chicago and London, 1965), 200.

Poetics have not yet reached agreement as to what Aristotle himself had intended.

Modern scholarship on Milton's preface has been preoccupied with the problem of ascertaining his sources. Verbal or doctrinal parallels have been noted in the works of Minturno, Guarini, Heinsius, and the Italian musician and theorist Monteverdi. Nevertheless, with the exception of studies by Sellin and Mueller, few efforts have been made to compare and evaluate these alleged sources. To assess their comparative merit as evidence lies beyond the scope of this essay. Most of the "key" concepts in Milton's remarks on catharsis were Renaissance commonplaces. The analogues hitherto noted in Minturno and other sixteenth-century theorists are less unconventional than they appeared to be a generation ago. The scholar should be reluctant to accept these, or other parallels he may discover, as evidence of Milton's positive indebtedness to a particular author.[2]

The rhetorical structure of the preface also needs to be explored. Far from being an ingenious, if cryptic, tissue of critical novelties or a systematic exposition of poetic theory, this "Epistle" is essentially a rhetorical document, an apology defending the poet's choice of genre and his preference for classical models over contemporary conventions. The preface is, in Milton's own words, a "self defence, or explanation," and its statements concerning catharsis (or any other subject) must be read and interpreted in this light.[3]

2. J. E. Spingarn, *A History of Literary Criticism in the Renaissance* (New York, 1925), 79–81; Allan H. Gilbert (ed.), *Literary Criticism: Plato to Dryden* (rpr. Detroit, 1962), 517, 593; Paul R. Sellin, "Sources of Milton's Catharsis: A Reconsideration," in James D. Simmonds (ed.), *Milton Studies in Honor of Harris Francis Fletcher* (Urbana, 1961), 104–22. See also Sellin, "Milton and Heinsius: Theoretical Homogeneity," in Rosario P. Armato and John M. Spalek (eds.), *Medieval Epic to the "Epic Theater" of Brecht* (Los Angeles, 1968), 125–34, and *Daniel Heinsius and Stuart England* (Leiden, 1968), 164–77; John Arthos, *Milton and the Italian Cities* (New York, 1968), 129–205; Martin Mueller, "Sixteenth-Century Italian Criticism and Milton's Theory of Catharsis," *Studies in English Literature*, VI (1966), 139–50, and "*Pathos* and *Katharsis* in *Samson Agonistes*," *ELH*, XXXI (1964), 156–74.

3. For rhetorical considerations underlying Milton's remarks on poetry and poetics in *The Reason of Church-Government*, see William Riley Parker, *Milton: A Biography* (2

71

MILTON'S REMARKS on catharsis occur within the immediate context of a defense of tragedy on the grounds of its dignity and utility, and within the larger context of an apologia for his own practice. Structurally, the preface falls into two divisions—a defense of tragedy itself and a defense of his own dramatic models. The two sections are linked, however, by the qualifying clause in the opening sentence: "Tragedy, as it was antiently compos'd, hath been ever held the gravest, moralest, and most profitable of all other Poems." In this way Milton made even his praise of tragedy contingent; its excellence was relative to the *stile antico*, to tragedy as the ancients composed it. This qualification, in turn, provided the foundation for his subsequent self-defense: "In the modelling therefore of this Poem, with good reason, the Antients and *Italians* are rather follow'd, as of much more authority and fame . . . of the style and uniformitie, and that commonly call'd the Plot . . . they only will best judge who are not unacquainted with *Aeschulus*, *Sophocles*, and *Euripides*, the three Tragic Poets unequall'd yet by any, and the best rule to all who endeavour to write Tragedy."[4]

His condemnation of the moderns provides a further link between the two parts of his essay; it effects the necessary transition between Milton's eulogy of tragedy as anciently composed and his defense of his own practice in following the ancients and the Italians: "This is mention'd to vindicate Tragedy from the small esteem, or rather infamy, which in the account of many it undergoes at this day with other common Interludes; hap'ning through the Poets error of intermixing Comic stuff with Tragic sadness and gravity; or introducing trivial and vulgar persons."

---

vols.; Oxford, 1968), I, 210. In Parker's opinion, Milton's brief autobiographical sketch, though "startling in its revealing irrelevance," is nonetheless "a subtle argument, designed to convince the nonconformist or Presbyterian reader that poetry has religious sanction."

4. As Sellin correctly observes, Milton treats "Aristotle's assertion . . . as a conditional statement. He says that Aristotle conceived of tragedy as effecting catharsis *because* tragedy (as constructed by the ancients) had always been considered the most serious, moral, and useful of poetic forms" ("Sources of Milton's Catharsis," in Simmonds (ed.), *Milton Studies*, 108–109). See *Complete Prose Works of John Milton* (New Haven and London, 1982), VIII, 133–37.

Like most apologies, moreover, Milton's preface includes both a *confirmatio* and a *refutatio*. The first comprises his citation of authorities and classical examples affirming the gravity and profitableness of tragedy. The second he has telescoped into a single sentence denouncing contemporary drama. Like most refutations, this rebuttal depends on a distinction in terms. The current indictments of tragedy spring, the poet argues, from its corruption by the moderns; in seeking popular appeal rather than tragic gravity, they have violated the cardinal principle of decorum. Such charges apply therefore only to the contemporary stage, not to ancient tragedies or (significantly) to modern tragedies modeled on those of the ancients. This argument was conventional; Milton had already employed it against contemporary poetasters in *The Reason of Church-Government*, Sidney had directed it against Elizabethan dramatists, and Lomazzo had turned it against contemporary painters.

Milton's *confirmatio* occupies the greater part of the first section. In this part of his defense he makes extensive use of the same type of arguments that other Renaissance apologists had employed in defending the arts and sciences. Like Bacon in *The Advancement of Learning* and Sidney in *An Apologie for Poetrie*; like Leonardo and Alberti and Lomazzo in their defenses of painting; or like Piccolomini in the "Proemio" to his *Annotationi . . . nel libro della poetica d'Aristotele*, Milton appeals to the conventional topics of *honestas* and *utilitas*.[5] He attempts to "vindicate" tragedy by emphasizing its dignity and profitableness—to counter the "small esteem" in which it is currently held, by demonstrating the high esteem bestowed on it by "gravest Writers" and "Men in highest dignity."

In confirmation of his initial statement or thesis he relies heavily on examples (a form of induction) and on the testimony of the ancients (a form of inartificial proof), adducing a list of authori-

5. See Cicero, *De Inventione*, trans. H. M. Hubbell (London and Cambridge, Mass., 1949), 324–27, on *honestas* and *utilitas* in deliberative oratory. The *Rhetorica ad Herennium*, on the other hand, treats *honestas* as a subdivision of *utilitas* (*Ad. C. Herennium de Ratione Dicendi*, trans. Harry Caplan [Cambridge, Mass., and London, 1954], 160–61).

73

ties that would normally seem disproportionate in so short an essay. These range from Scripture (a Pauline epistle and the Book of Revelation) to pagan worthies (Dionysius, Cicero, Augustus Caesar, Seneca, Plutarch) and "a Father of the Church" (Gregory Nazianzen). It is within this context that the allusion to Aristotle occurs; it is a part—indeed the most important part—of the *confirmatio*. Introduced specifically to support the general statement that precedes it, it is designed primarily to demonstrate the gravity, morality, and utility of tragedy rather than to set forth a theory of tragic effect.

Aristotle's name heads the list, and Milton devotes considerably more space to his opinion than to those of other authorities. For several reasons this reference was especially vital for Milton's rhetorical strategy. Not only was Aristotle the principal authority on tragedy, he was also virtually the only classical philosopher who ranked with Plato and could refute the latter's indictment of tragedy; he could therefore serve as a useful ally against possible opponents—adversaries of the drama who might support their condemnation by appealing to *The Republic*.

In considering Milton's remarks on tragic effect, one should bear in mind the following points. In the first place, they are subordinated to the principal intent of his apologia—to defend his own practice. The doctrine of "purgation" is instrumental to his rhetorical strategy only insofar as it enables him to argue the gravity and profitableness of tragedy "as it was antiently compos'd." (He does not even mention the Greek term *katharsis*; instead he employs the Latin equivalent *lustratio*—in the epigraph to his work—and the English verb form *purge* in the text itself.)

In the second place, his remarks on this subject are partial; they attempt neither a comprehensive definition of tragedy nor a balanced statement of tragic effect. Elsewhere he alludes, in fact, to the role of dramatic action in arousing the passions, and to the interconnection between passion and thought (*dianoia*): "whatsoever hath passion or admiration in all the changes of that which is call'd fortune from without, or the wily subtleties and refluxes of mans thoughts from within."[6] This allusion to for-

6. John Milton, *The Reason of Church-Government Urged Against Prelaty*, in Don M.

tune's "changes" clearly refers to the tragic incidents portrayed in the fable—a point especially vital in Aristotle's theory of tragedy, but omitted in the preface to *Samson Agonistes*. Milton obviously held a broader view of tragic effect than the preface alone appears to indicate. As he recognized, the proper "delight" of tragedy arose not only from imitation of the passions but also from imitation of an action. Indeed the epigraph on the title page begins with Aristotle's definition of tragedy as μίμησις πράξεως σπουδαίας, "imitatio actionis seriae."

The remarks in the preface provide a severely limited selection rather than a representative summary of Milton's views on tragic effect; and the basis of this selection appears to have been primarily rhetorical. To regard his preface as a miniature treatise on poetics rather than a brief defense of his own practice is to mistake its genre. To interpret his observations as an epitome of his tragic doctrine is to mistake the part for the whole.

The third point to keep in mind is that the novelty of Milton's statements on tragic effect has been greatly exaggerated. The principal features of his discussion of purgation—the imitation of the passions, their reduction to "just measure" instead of complete eradication, the analogy between poetry and medicine—have numerous parallels in the critical treatises of the period. Finally, the particular aspects of tragic purgation that Milton selects for emphasis may have been chosen partly for their relevance to the principal argument commonly directed against tragedy—that it excites the passions and is therefore morally dangerous.

HAVING BRIEFLY examined the context of Milton's statement, let us return to the text itself. Tragedy is "said by *Aristotle* to be of power by raising pity and fear, or terror, to purge the mind of those and such like passions, that is to temper and reduce them to just measure with a kind of delight, stirr'd up by reading or seeing those passions well imitated." In support of Aristotle's "assertion" Milton then turns to medicine for an analogous kind of purgation: "for so in Physic things of melancholic hue and quality are

---

Wolfe (ed.), *Complete Prose Works of John Milton* (New Haven, 1952), I, 817, hereafter cited as *Yale Prose*.

us'd against melancholy, sowr against sowr, salt to remove salt humours."

To modern observers this passage obviously contains much more (and much less) than was actually "said by *Aristotle.*" It confronts us, accordingly, with several interrelated problems. First, how well did Milton understand Aristotle? How far does this passage reflect views explicitly stated in the *Poetics*? And how far is it merely a Renaissance gloss, derived from earlier commentators or from Milton's own study of the treatise? Second, what are the sources of the "non-Aristotelian" elements in this passage? Third, how much of this passage did Milton intend to represent as Aristotelian statement—as actually "said by *Aristotle*"—and how much is his own commentary or exposition on Aristotle's text? Although these questions cannot yet receive definitive answers, they are not unanswerable. Thanks to the research of previous scholars, we may perhaps approach a tentative solution.

The first part of Milton's statement offers little difficulty. That tragedy is "of power by raising pity and fear . . . to purge the mind of those and such like passions" seems, on the whole, a fairly accurate paraphrase of the Aristotelian definition translated on the title page of Milton's drama: "Per misericordiam & metum perficiens talium affectuum lustrationem." Except for its reference to "the mind," Milton's statement is a faithful rendering of what was explicitly "said by *Aristotle*"—perhaps, indeed, more faithful than most modern translations.

Nevertheless, whatever Aristotle actually "said" in this passage, he clearly left much more *un*said. His brief definition of tragedy did not specify how or why it accomplished its catharsis; and his commentators were quick to remedy his omission. They debated whether all or only a few of the passions were to be purged; whether the emotions purged were identical with those that effected the purgation; whether the passions were to be eradicated entirely or merely moderated and reduced to "just measure." They glossed this passage in the *Poetics* with others from the same work, with the discussion of "purgative melodies" in the *Politics*, and with medical theory. Although some of the interpretations they imposed on the text may seem exaggerated when judged by twentieth-century interpretations of Aristotle, these critics nevertheless arrived at such views by well-tried exegetical methods. Their deficiencies can be partly attributed to the aims and techniques of Renaissance scholarship itself.

The essential difficulty for the twentieth-century reader lies not in Milton's paraphrase of Aristotle, but in his own gloss on his Aristotelian paraphrase. This is his own exegesis (albeit an incomplete exegesis) of a notoriously ambiguous passage in the *Poetics*; as such it does not pretend to be what was actually "said by *Aristotle*" but what the commentator thought Aristotle meant by what he *did* say; it is Milton's attempt to resolve an ambiguity that he and many others had encountered in the text, to explain how and why tragedy achieves its *lustratio*, or purgation.

His statement that tragedy is able "to temper and reduce them [*i.e.*, the passions] to just measure with a kind of delight, stirr'd up by reading or seeing those passions well imitated" is essentially his own gloss on the Aristotelian text he has just paraphrased. It could, accordingly (as he well knew), seem plausible only insofar as it did not contradict the text itself. Before analyzing his gloss, therefore, let us turn first to the text and to his translation and paraphrase.

According to late nineteenth- and twentieth-century interpretations of the *Poetics*, the tragic emotions are essentially the product of events. Arising out of the development of the fable, they result from the dramatist's skill in plotting and his mastery of dramatic structure. The fable itself the "soul" of the poem—is an imitation of an action; and from the evolution and unraveling of this action, in accordance with verisimilitude and probability, the poem derives its emotional force. Character and thought – *ethos* and *dianoia*—are secondary to plot; to the latter belong the three elements principally responsible for tragic effect—reversal, discovery, and suffering (*peripeteia, anagnorisis, pathos*).

Such an interpretation appears to be justified by the strong emphasis that Aristotle places on the fable (*mythos*) throughout his treatise; but it is not explicitly stated in the phrase that Milton translates on the title page, paraphrases near the beginning of his preface, and proceeds in due order to explicate. Elsewhere in the *Poetics* Aristotle stresses the types of action most suitable for arousing pity and fear, but his statement on catharsis makes no mention of "deeds" or "actions" as the means of exciting these emotions. More than one translator, however, regarded this meaning as implicit in Aristotle's statement and accordingly introduced it into his own translation. Bywater, for instance, renders this passage as "with incidents arousing pity and fear, wherewith to accomplish its catharsis of such emotions." The word *incidents* does not, however, occur in Aristotle's text (δι' ἐλέου καὶ φόβου περαίνουσα τὴν τῶν τοιούτων παθημάτων κάθαρσιν). Earlier, as Bywater acknowledged, Goulston had advanced a similar interpretation, inserting the qualifying phrase "factis expressum" after the words "per Misericordiam, Metumque"; but he had placed his own addition in italics to indicate that the reference to "deeds" did not occur in the text. His version of the *Poetics* was not only a literal translation; it was also, in a sense, a paraphrase.[7]

Bywater's translation would, of course, tend to rule out Milton's interpretation; but in actuality Milton's translation ("Per misericordiam & metum perficiens talium affectuum lustrationem") is closer to Aristotle's actual words than is Bywater's rendering. The text, as he renders it, retains its original ambiguity and is therefore capable of multiple interpretations—including the meaning he ascribes to it in his own paraphrase and explanation.

Although Renaissance commentators sometimes showed considerable freedom in paraphrasing and explaining Aristotle's text and in elaborating their own definitions of tragedy after his precedent, they usually strove for strict verbal accuracy in translating his text and they generally preserved the distinction between a literal translation and a paraphrase. Goulston, as we have observed, italicized his own additions. Other commentators—Maggi, Robortello, Castelvetro—might advance very different theories of trag-

7. Aristotle, *On the Art of Poetry*, ed. and trans. Ingram Bywater (Oxford, 1909), 16–17; Theodorus Goulston, *Aristotelis de Poetica Liber, Latinè Conversus, et Analytica* [sic] *Methodo Illustratus* (London, 1623), 11–12; compare Aristotle, *On the Art of Poetry*, ed. and trans. Bywater, 151; Sellin, "Sources of Milton's Catharsis," in Simmonds (ed.), *Milton Studies*, 118. Bywater interprets Aristotle's phrase as meaning "practically . . . 'by piteous and alarming scenes.'"

edy and hold highly divergent views as to how Aristotle's text ought to be interpreted, but they normally differentiated their own paraphrases or explanations from the text itself. Maggi, for instance, reproduced Pazzi's translation of this passage, "per misericordiam verò atque terrorem perturbationes huiusmodi purgans," and then added his own (and Lombardi's) "explanation" and finally his own "annotations" or commentary. Robortello likewise accepted Pazzi's translation as the basis for his own commentary. Castelvetro rendered the same passage as "induca per misericordia, & per ispavento purgatione di così fatte passioni" and then proceeded to advance, in his commentary, a theory of tragedy that is in several respects radically different from that of his predecessors.[8] In Milton's approach to Aristotle we encounter a similar regard for verbal accuracy in translating the words of the text, and a similar freedom in explaining them. He provides us first with a literal translation, then with a paraphrase, and finally with a brief explanation or commentary.

His paraphrase of what was "said by *Aristotle*" is less accurate than his translation, but it is still considerably less free than the paraphrases written by many of his predecessors and nearcontemporaries. The first addition he makes to Aristotle's text in paraphrasing it is his allusion to "the mind." This was scarcely a major addition, and perhaps he felt it advisable in view of the notorious ambiguity of the word *pathēma* and its equivalents "passion" and "perturbation." His qualification, moreover, had already become a commonplace in Aristotelian commentary. Goulston had employed the same word (again in italics to indicate that it represented his own addition), "eiusmodi *vehementes animorum*

8. Vincenzo Maggi, *Vincentii Madii Brixiani et Bartholomaei Lombardi Veronensis in Aristotelis Librum de Poetica Communes Explanationes: Madii Vero in Eundem Librum Propriae Annotationes* (Venice, 1550), 96 (hereafter cited as *Explanationes*). According to Girolamo Tiraboschi, *Storia della Letteratura Italiana* (13 vols.; Milan, 1824), XIII, 2156, Lombardi had been "surprised by immature death" and Maggi had continued the work alone, adding notes and comments "written in the manner of those times, that is, explicating Aristotle with passages from other ancient writers, and basing precepts more on authority than on reason and nature." *Francisci Robortelli Utinensis in Librum Aristotelis de Arte Poetica Explicationes* (Florence, 1548), 52 (hereafter cited as *Explicationes*); Lodovico Castelvetro, *Poetica d'Aristotele vulgarizzata, et sposta* (Basel, 1576), 113.

Perturbationes"; and Maggi and Lombardi had introduced it into their own "explanation" of the text: "MISERICORDIAM VERÒ ATQUE TERROREM PERTURBATIONES HUIUSMODI PURGANS: hoc est animum liberans à perturbationibus, misericordiae & terrori similibus."[9]

The second addition Milton makes is more substantial. The word *those* ("those and such like passions") does not occur in the text he is paraphrasing. On the contrary, Aristotle employed only the ambiguous term τοιούτων (which Milton renders as "talium" and "such like"), and thereby gave rise to one of the major debates in Cinquecento criticism. Which of the emotions does tragedy attempt to purge? Granted that it arouses pity and fear, does it also *purge* them—or does it arouse them only to purge other, more harmful emotions? Does catharsis apply only to pity and fear? does it exclude pity and fear? or does it comprehend a variety of emotions including pity and fear?[10]

On this issue critics were divided. Maggi, for instance, explicitly denied that the end of tragedy could be the purgation of pity and fear, for these emotions could, in his opinion, have highly beneficial results. His view was that tragedy employs pity and fear to purge the mind of other, more harmful passions, wrath, avarice, and lust (*luxuria*). For these reasons, Maggi maintains, Aristotle did not regard the end of tragedy to be purging the human mind of terror and pity. Instead, he regarded its end as using these emotions to remove other perturbations from the mind. By this expulsion, the mind is adorned with virtues. Thus when wrath is driven out, there succeeds gentleness. When avarice is expelled, there succeeds liberality. "His itaque rationibus haudquaquam dubito, Aristotelem nolle Tragoediae finem esse animam humanam à terrore misericordiave expurgare; sed his uti ad alias perturbationes ab animo removendas: ex quarum remotione animus virtutibus

9. Goulston, *Aristotelis de Poetica*, 11–12; Sellin, "Sources of Milton's Catharsis," in Simmonds (ed.), *Milton Studies*, 118; Maggi, *Explanationes*, 97. Maggi notes, "What the Greeks call *pathos*, we call passion ('affectum'), or perturbation of mind" (50, my translation, as are all others unless otherwise noted).

10. Spingarn, *History of Literary Criticism*, 74–81; Bernard Weinberg, *A History of Literary Criticism in the Italian Renaissance* (2 vols.; Chicago, 1961); see also Sellin, "Sources of Milton's Catharsis," in Simmonds (ed.), *Milton Studies*, 111–15.

exornatur. nam ira, verbi gratia, depulsa, succedit mansuetudo. expulsa avaritia, inducitur liberalitas. atque ita de caeteris."[11]

Piccolomini, on the other hand, denies that pity and fear are excluded from purgation. Surveying the eleven passions of the mind discussed in Aristotle's *Rhetoric* (five belonging to the irascible faculty and six to the concupiscible appetite), he declared that tragedy arouses pity and fear by portraying grievous events that have befallen great persons and thereby purges and liberates the mind from excess of emotions (*affetti*). Pity and fear are included in this purgation, inasmuch as tragedy tempers fear and moderates pity. Castelvetro, in turn, explicitly asserts that tragedy utilizes pity and fear to purge "these passions" and drive them from the heart. By "its example and its frequent representation" of things worthy of pity, fear, and cowardice (*viltà*), it confers magnanimity on an ignoble audience, lends courage to fearful men, and makes compassionate men severe. Tragedy diminishes fear and pity by accustoming the spectator to fearful and pitiable objects—just as in a pestilence pity and fear are stirred by the first few deaths, but cease after hundreds and thousands have perished. If "terrible and pitiable actions are uncommon they move men the more to terror and to compassion, but if they are less frequent they move them the less, and because of their frequency are able to purge the terror and compassion of mortal lives." Guarini similarly insists that tragedy purges pity and fear ("terror purges terror") but draws a sharp distinction between good and evil aspects of these emotions. The "terror of internal death . . . excited in the spirit of the spectator by the image of what is represented, interprets the injurious evil tendency as a calamity"; but reason, "abhorring the bad tendency . . . drives it out, leaving behind only the beneficial fear of infamy and of internal death, which is the foundation of virtue."[12]

11. Maggi, *Explanationes*, 98.

12. *Annotationi di M Alessandro Piccolomini nel libro della poetica d'Aristotele* (Venice, 1575), 102–103; Castelvetro, *Poetica d'Aristotele*, 117; Gilbert (ed.), *Literary Criticism*, 315–16, 517. See Weinberg, *History of Literary Criticism*, I, 627, on Giacomini's lectures about catharsis. These summarized three different theories of tragic purgation—that tragedy purges only pity and fear; that it purges the *opposites* of these passions; that it "moderates" *all* the passions through its spectacle of "the instability of human affairs"—

Against this background Milton's additions to Aristotle's assertion seem modest indeed. He does, to be sure, introduce into his
paraphrase two concepts that are not explicitly stated in the passage he is paraphrasing; in the eyes of some of his predecessors,
moreover, one of these would scarcely have seemed even implicit.
By inserting the word *those* into his paraphrase, he took a positive
stand against commentators who, like Maggi, had dogmatically
denied that tragedy purges pity and fear. Unlike many Cinquecento critics, Milton does not elaborate this point into a systematic theory or qualify it by new and novel distinctions. He does
not endeavor to define and catalog "such like passions" or to distinguish between the beneficial and injurious modes of pity and
terror. In comparison with theorists like Castelvetro and Guarini,
the views expressed in the paraphrase and in the brief *explicatio*
that follows it are conservative.

Except for two insertions—one of them a commonplace, the
other a debatable but widely accepted interpretation—Milton's
paraphrase is an accurate restatement of the passage he had already
translated literally on the title page. Thus far he has not been unfaithful to what was actually "said by *Aristotle.*"

As THE PASSAGE that follows this initial statement has sometimes
proved a stumbling block for modern critics, let us consider first
its general nature and function and then examine some of its basic
ideas. Strictly speaking, it is not a *paraphrase*, but a commentary.
It amplifies and elucidates the statement in the Greek text and in
Milton's own paraphrase. It is an explication of Aristotle's dictum
rather than a restatement.

The five principal ideas advanced in this explication, moreover—moderation rather than extirpation of the passions; imitation as the source of tragic delight; delight as an attendant of
purgation; the imitation of the passions; and the medical analogy—are by no means novel additions to Renaissance critical

---

and offered a fourth explanation, that the passions are "purged by exteriorization."
Mueller calls attention to the "very striking" resemblance between Milton's views and
Giacomini's ideas on "general politics," the "theory of moderation," and the combina-
tion of "purgation with tragic delight" ("Sixteenth-Century Italian Criticism," 148).

thought. They had already become familiar and even widespread doctrines in neo-Aristotelian theory. All of them had found plausible, though still debatable, support in the works of Aristotle— his *Ethics*, *Politics*, and *Rhetoric* as well as his *Poetics*. In varying degrees, these concepts had become part of the Renaissance Aristotelian tradition; few Cinquecento critics would have regarded any of the five as either novel or "un-Aristotelian." Some of them, indeed, had become near-commonplaces.

In declaring that tragedy may "temper and reduce" the passions "to just measure," Milton commits himself, once again, to a positive stand on an old controversy. The question of the degree of purgation—whether tragedy effected a total or merely partial reduction of the passions—was another of the highly debatable issues arising out of the ambiguities of Aristotle's text. In asserting the latter view, Milton advances essentially the same interpretation that he had expressed earlier in *The Reason of Church-Government*: poetry can "allay the perturbations of the mind, and set the affections in right tune."[13] This conception was by no means rare in Renaissance criticism; nor could it be regarded as un-Aristotelian. Although it is never explicitly stated in the *Poetics*, it is nevertheless consistent with views expressed in the *Nicomachean Ethics* as to the nature of the passions and their relation to virtue and vice. Moreover, it was consistent with Milton's own views on this subject. For Milton as for Aristotle, virtue consisted in a mean or "just measure" between extremes. For both, the passions or affections constituted the common subject matter of vice and virtue. Other philosophical schools—notably the Stoics and certain Neo-Pythagorean or Neoplatonic philosophers—regarded a complete eradication of the passions as essential for perfect virtue, but the ataraxy of the Stoic sage and the passionless perfection of the Neoplatonic *anima purgata* were, on the whole, alien to Renaissance Aristotelianism and indeed to Christian humanism.

One of the strongest arguments for this interpretation, then,

---

13. Milton, *The Reason of Church-Government*, in *Yale Prose*, I, 816–17. For poetry's ability to "temper" the affections and set them in "right tune," see Aristotle's remarks on the power of music: "There seems to be in us a sort of affinity to musical modes and rhythms, which makes some philosophers say that the soul is a tuning, others, that it

seems to be its fidelity to Aristotelian ethics.[14] The alternative view, which regarded tragic purgation as the complete eradication of the passions, would fit a Stoic or Neo-Pythagorean ethical system but would hardly accord with the moral principles of the Peripatetics. Several of Milton's predecessors, moreover, had emphasized this point, affirming that catharsis denoted an Aristotelian moderation of the passions, not the total eradication demanded by the Stoics.

For Piccolomini, the principal end of tragedy (as of all other species of poetry) is utility or instruction, delight serving merely as a secondary aim and as a means to the principal end. The greatest utility, he continues, is to possess a true tranquillity of mind. As such tranquillity cannot be stained or disturbed except by the flow of passions through the mind, tragedy is most useful insofar as it moderates the emotions and thereby fosters peace of mind. Distinguishing sharply between Stoic and Peripatetic conceptions of the passions and their relation to tranquillity, Piccolomini observes that the latter school does not regard total eradication of the emotions as a prerequisite of tranquillity. For the Peripatetics, it is enough to purge, moderate, and reduce them to a certain "good temperament." The rule and measure of this purgation or "tempering" belong to reason; when the passions conform to reason, they are said to be "moderated" and purged.[15]

Guarini similarly observes that "the word *purge* has two meanings. One means *to blot out completely*"; the second sense, however,

possesses tuning" (*Politica*, trans. Benjamin Jowett, in *The Basic Works of Aristotle*, ed. Richard McKeon [New York, 1941], 1312).

14. Aristotle, *Ethica Nicomachea*, trans. W. D. Ross, in *The Basic Works of Aristotle*: "Virtue must have the quality of aiming at the intermediate. I mean moral virtue; for it is this that is concerned with passions and actions" (958). See also 954, 956.

15. Piccolomini, *Annotationi*, 101–102. See Spingarn, *History of Literary Criticism*, on Sperone Speroni's conviction that "Aristotle cannot refer to the complete eradication of pity and fear—a conception which is Stoic rather than Peripatetic, for Aristotle does not require to free ourselves from emotions, but to regulate them, since in themselves they are not bad" (81); and Weinberg, *History of Literary Criticism*, on Borghesi's belief that poetry is "moderatrice de trasandanti affetti" (I, 343). Quoting Heinsius' statement that "defectum quoque eorum atque excessum expiant ac purgant. mediocritatem verò . . . relinquunt," Sellin adds that "Milton could find in Heinsius an elaborate version of Aristotle's mean systematically applied to the *Poetics*" ("Sources of Milton's Catharsis," in Simmonds [ed.], *Milton Studies*, 120).

"does not mean to blot out . . . but to rid . . . of all vileness and make [a thing] perfect in its nature. In this second sense is to be taken the *purge* of tragedy, as also the physicians take it. . . . A tragic poem . . . does not purge the affections in Stoic fashion, by removing them totally from our hearts, but by moderating and reducing them to that proper consistency which can contribute to a virtuous habit." Pity and fear "need to be purged, that is, reduced to a proper mixture, and this is done by tragedy." [16]

In elucidating obscure or ambiguous passages in the *Poetics*, Renaissance commentators not uncommonly sought clarification from other writings by the same author. To explain Aristotle's theory of purgation, Cinquecento critics ransacked the *Ethics*, the *Rhetoric*, and the *Politics* for the philosopher's views (relevant or irrelevant) on the passions. Maggi, for instance, explained the word *pathē* (which occurs near the beginning of the *Poetics*) in terms of Aristotle's ethical theory. All emotions, Maggi declares, are the matter of virtues, and the rational part of the soul is engaged in moderating them. Although it conduces to a mean in restraining them, it creates the habits of the virtues in the mind. "Sunt autem affectus omnes, virtutum materiae quaedam, circa quarum moderationem rationalis animae pars versatur: quae dum eosdem fraenans, ad mediocritatem ducit, virtutum habitus omnes in animo procreat." [17]

In a more modest—and perhaps more sensible—way, this is precisely what Milton has done in his preface. He has glossed an obscure passage in the *Poetics* with concepts derived from the *Ethics* and (as we shall see later) from the *Politics*. He explains Aristotle's poetic doctrine—the purgation of the passions—by citing the ethical doctrine advanced by the same author—the moderation of the passions. By reducing the emotions to "just measure," tragedy performs an ethical function comparable to that of reason itself; like reason, it governs the passions and thereby serves as an

---

16. Gilbert (ed.), *Literary Criticism*, 516–17. Gilbert calls attention to the parallel between Guarini's phrase "ridotti a vertuoso temperamento" and Milton's "to temper and reduce them to just measure" (517*n*), but Sellin observes that "having thus reviewed this idea, Guarini *rejects* it and turns back to the first alternative (extirpate catharsis)" ("Sources of Milton's Catharsis," in Simmonds [ed.], *Milton Studies*, 115–16).

17. Maggi, *Explanationes*, 51.

agent of moral virtue. This argument, needless to say, is vital to Milton's rhetorical strategy, for it supports, and demonstrates, his initial thesis. To prove that tragedy is indeed the "moralest" of all other poems he turns appropriately to the central thesis of the standard treatise on moral philosophy, the *Nicomachean Ethics*.

Milton's observation on the origin and function of tragic delight is by no means new, but the tradition behind it is complex and requires some elucidation. Like many of his contemporaries and predecessors, he has clearly subordinated delight to utility; pleasure serves the graver, moral ends of tragedy. This view, of course, antedates the Renaissance Aristotelian tradition; it is essentially an inheritance from classical rhetoric with its threefold end—to teach, delight, and move—and from Horatian poetics with its dual emphasis on utility and delight. From Horace's injunction to mix the *utile* and *dulce* and from his statement that poets ought to aim either at instruction or at pleasure ("aut prodesse volunt aut delectare poetae"), medieval and Renaissance poetics had evolved the ideal of poetry as a mode of delightful teaching, a form of instruction all the more effective because it employed pleasure in order to teach and to persuade. Delight served the end of utility. The poet combined the *utile* of moral doctrine with the *dulce* of verse, rhetorical ornament, or invented fable. In rhetorical terms, the poem served as inductive proof; it was a moral or political exemplum.[18]

The rediscovery of Aristotle's *Poetics* might force a reappraisal of well-established poetic theories, but on the whole it did not displace them. Instead, neo-Aristotelian theory tended to absorb them or (by introducing new and partially understood concepts) to stimulate them to new developments; in this way it gave them a new vitality, a second youth. The traditional subordination of delight to utility remained, but with a wider application. The traditional sources of poetic *delight* were broadened by adding Aris-

18. For the syncretistic methodology of Renaissance criticism and the influence of Horace on interpretations of Aristotle, see Weinberg, "From Aristotle to Pseudo-Aristotle," in Olson (ed.), *Aristotle's "Poetics,"* 199–200; Weinberg, *History of Literary Criticism*; Marvin T. Herrick, *The Fusion of Horatian and Aristotelian Criticism, 1531–1555* (Urbana, 1946).

totelian interpretations of imitation. The conventional ideas of poetic *utility* were enriched by the Aristotelian doctrine of catharsis. Thus in Tasso's "Allegory" to the *Gerusalemme Liberata* one finds a fusion of Aristotelian and medieval poetics: "Heroic poetry is composed of imitation and allegory, like an animal in which two natures are conjoined. With the former it allures to itself the minds and ears of men, and delights them marvellously. With the latter it instructs them in virtue or in knowledge, or in both." In the opening stanzas of his epic, however, he returns to the older conception of poetry as delightful teaching. "Truth convey'd in verse of gentle kind" is like a sweetened medicine administered to sick children:

> Anoint with sweets the vessel's foremost parts,
> To make them taste the potions sharp we give;
> They drink deceived; and so deceiv'd they live.[19]

In Renaissance discussions of the nature and ends of the poetic art, it is not uncommon, therefore, to find a mixture of Aristotelian and medieval concepts. In Varchi, Mazzoni, Minturno, Tasso, Sidney, and numerous other critics, one encounters definitions of poetry that have been partially modeled on Aristotle's definition of tragedy but which nevertheless incorporate the traditional twofold or threefold "ends" of poetry inherited from the Horatian and Ciceronian traditions. These specifically define the ends of poetry as delight, instruction, and, in those cases where the critic has been most strongly influenced by rhetorical theory, persuasion. In most of these cases, moreover, delight is clearly subordinated to utility—to instructing and moving the poet's audience.[20]

This subordination of delight to utility could find at least a limited textual support in Aristotle's own works. Besides subordinating poetics to ethics, and ethics to politics, he had argued that mu-

---

19. See also the combination of delight and utility in Antonio Posio's view of catharsis (Weinberg, *History of Literary Criticism*, I, 17); Torquato Tasso, "Allegoria della *Gerusalemme Liberata*," in *Le Prose diverse di Torquato Tasso*, ed. Cesare Guasti (2 vols.; Florence, 1875), I, 301; Torquato Tasso, *Jerusalem Delivered*, trans. Edward Fairfax, ed. John Charles Nelson (New York, n.d.), 2 (Book I, stanza 3).

20. For Minturno's definition, see Gilbert (ed.), *Literary Criticism*, 377–85.

sic may have a nobler "use" than pleasure. "In addition to this common pleasure," he had declared in his *Politics*, "felt and shared in by all (for the pleasure given by music is natural, and therefore adapted to all ages and characters), may it not have also some influence over the character and the soul? It must have such an influence if characters are affected by it." Even "in mere melodies there is an imitation of character, for the musical modes differ essentially from one another, and those who hear them are differently affected by each." Music has therefore "a power of forming the character, and should therefore be introduced into the education of the young." Even that time-honored cliché—the conception of poetry as a sugared medicine, making instruction palatable through delight—could derive support from the *Politics*: "The study [of music] is suited to the stage of youth, for young persons will not, if they can help, endure anything which is not sweetened by music, and music has a natural sweetness."[21]

The conception of delight as a secondary end of poetry—both subordinate and instrumental to utility—was, then, thoroughly conventional in Renaissance criticism; and it was within this framework that Milton (like many of his predecessors) interpreted the Aristotelian concepts of mimesis and catharsis. Imitation was delightful; purgation was morally useful. In treating the delight aroused by imitation as an assisting cause in achieving catharsis, Milton was adapting the ideas he encountered in the *Poetics* to a frame of reference already standard in Renaissance thought. He was, in effect, subordinating delight to utility.

In regarding pleasure as subservient to usefulness, he was in fundamental agreement with the majority of Renaissance critics. Few of them shared Castelvetro's opinion that delight alone was the principal end of tragedy. Some of them specifically linked neo-Aristotelian concepts of imitation with older theories concerning the poetic or rhetorical exemplum. Many of them regarded poetics as the handmaid of moral and civil philosophy—or indeed of theology—and accordingly stressed the ethical, political, and religious functions of tragedy.

Milton's allusion to the "delight" stirred up by tragic imitation

21. Aristotle, *Politics*, 1311–12.

would have raised few eyebrows among his contemporaries; Aristotle himself had declared that it is "natural for all to delight in works of imitation." Moreover, Milton's further suggestion—that such delight might actually assist purgation—was not uncommon, even though many of his predecessors held sharply divergent views on this subject. In the *Politics*, they observed, Aristotle had discussed the influence of the so-called purgative melodies on "feelings such as pity and fear"—the very emotions excited by tragedy—in terms that clearly associated purgation with delight: "Some persons fall into a religious frenzy, whom we see as a result of the sacred melodies—when they have used the melodies that excite the soul to mystic frenzy—restored as though they had found healing and purgation. Those who are influenced by pity and fear, and every emotional nature, must have a like experience, and others in so far as each is susceptible to such emotions, and all are in a manner purged, and their souls lightened and delighted." [22]

The context as well as the contents of this passage made it a convenient gloss on the text of the *Poetics*. Preceded by an extensive discussion of music as imitation of character and passion and followed by the recommendation that "purgative melodies" should be performed at the theater inasmuch as they "give an innocent pleasure to mankind," this passage seemed equally relevant to the drama. Moreover, it appeared to provide a foundation for several of the principal commonplaces of "pre-Aristotelian" poetic theory—the combination of utility with delight and the analogy between poetry and medicine. Maggi quoted it to elucidate Aristotle's definition of tragedy, specifically noting its parallel between musical and medical catharsis and its emphasis on utility and pleasure. In his version one encounters, indeed, some of the very *topoi* that Milton himself subsequently employed—concepts that had not been explicitly stated in Aristotle's definition of tragedy but that were nevertheless read into it by critics familiar with the *Politics*. [23]

First, Milton alludes to the power of tragedy "to purge the

---

22. Aristotle, *On the Art of Poetry*, ed. and trans. Bywater, 9; Aristotle, *Politics*, 1315.
23. Aristotle, *Politics*, 1311–12, 1315; Maggi, *Explanationes*, 98.

mind." The word *mind* (as we have seen) does not occur in the relevant passage in the *Poetics*, but it does appear in the analogous passage in the *Politics* ("animum . . . expiant"). Second, Milton asserts that tragedy purges pity and fear ("those . . . passions"). In the *Poetics* this idea may be implied, but is not explicitly stated; for many Renaissance critics, Aristotle's term τῶν τοιούτων was ambiguous, and the precise identity of the emotions to be purged was subject to doubt. The *Politics*, on the other hand, refers *explicitly* to the purgation of pity and fear as well as to other emotions: "quod idem pati necesse est eos, & qui commiseratione, & qui metu, & generatim sunt affecti" ("Those who are influenced by pity and fear, and every emotional nature, must have a like experience"). Third, although the medical parallel, so common in Renaissance poetic theory, does not occur in the account of catharsis provided by the *Poetics*, it *does* appear in the political treatise: "idoneumque reddunt . . . carminibusque ita constitui, ut si medicinam, purgationemque reperissent" ("as a result of the sacred melodies . . . restored as though they had found healing and purgation").

Finally, Milton alludes to purgation "with a kind of delight." The definition of tragedy given in the *Poetics* makes no mention of pleasure as accompanying catharsis, though such a view may be implicit in other sections of the treatise. The *Politics*, on the other hand, offers a close verbal parallel: "omnesque aliqua ex parte purgari, & allevari cum voluptate" ("and all are in a manner purged, and their souls lightened and delighted").[24]

Milton's remarks on tragic purgation seem, on the whole, to represent a conflation of Aristotle's definition of tragedy with opinions on catharsis advanced in the *Politics*. These he amplified and explained, in turn, with doctrines likewise derived from Aristotelian sources—the moderation of the passions, from the *Ethics*; imitation of the passions, from the *Poetics* and the *Politics* alike; mimesis as the source of pleasure, from the *Poetics*. The medical analogy, explicit but still undeveloped in the *Politics*, he elaborated as other critics had done before him.

24. Maggi, *Explanationes*, 98. The phrase *cum voluptate* is, of course, a literal translation of Aristotle's expression *meth' hedones*. See Bernardo Segni, *Trattato de' Governi d'Aristotile*, ed. Cesare Bini (Milan, 1864), 208, for his version of the same passage.

Milton's expression "with a kind of delight" is not entirely free from ambiguity. Does it mean that purgation is accomplished "by aid of" pleasure, or merely "accompanied with" pleasure, or both? A similar ambiguity is inherent in the *Politics*. Aristotle's phrase μεθ᾽ ἡδονῆς ("with delight") could mean both "by aid of" and "in conjunction with"; the Latin equivalent *cum voluptate* was likewise ambiguous. Whichever meaning Milton intended (and it is quite possible that he may not have recognized the ambiguity or else did not want to split hairs over this point), his interpretation could hardly be regarded as original.[25]

On the relationship between tragic purgation and tragic pleasure Renaissance critics held sharply divergent views; some regarded purgation as "accompanied with" pleasure, others as accomplished "by means of" delight. On the one hand, for instance, Giacomini (in a passage clearly influenced by the *Politics*) maintained that "this lightening or purgation of the soul is accompanied by a feeling of pleasure." On the other hand, Denores declared that pleasure serves as the instrument or agent of catharsis; poetry endeavors to purge the listeners "col mezzo del diletto da' più importanti affetti dell' animo." Whichever meaning Milton meant to signify by his phrase ("with . . . delight"), his interpretation appears to be thoroughly traditional.[26]

In asserting that tragic pleasure springs from imitation, Milton was partly following Aristotle's doctrine that "the tragic pleasure is that of pity and fear, and the poet has to produce it by a work of imitation." There is nevertheless one significant difference between them: whereas Aristotle stresses the actions or "incidents" imitated in the story, Milton emphasizes the "passions . . . imi-

25. Several earlier critics regarded delight as an effect or by-product of catharsis, but Milton explicitly asserts that imitation is the cause of tragic pleasure. Castelvetro, unlike Milton, held that by "delight" Aristotle meant purgation—the expulsion from the human mind of pity and fear by means of these very emotions (*Poetica d'Aristotele*, 299). See Henry George Liddell and Robert Scott (eds.), *A Greek-English Lexicon* (rev. ed.; Oxford, 1925–40), on the preposition *meta* ("with"): with the genitive, it signifies "*in the midst of, among, between*"; or "*in common, along with, by aid of*" (implying a closer union than *syn*)"; or "*in conjunction with.*" See B. L. Gildersleeve and Gonzales Lodge (eds.), *Gildersleeve's Latin Grammar* (3d ed.; Boston, [*ca.* 1894]), nos. 392, 399, on *cum* as ablative of attendance and as ablative of manner.

26. Giacomini and Denores quoted in Weinberg, *History of Literary Criticism*, I, 627, 625; see Mueller, "Sixteenth-Century Italian Criticism," 148.

tated." In the context of Renaissance poetic theory, however, this divergence would have appeared less glaring; in the eyes of many Cinquecento critics (as will be discussed later), Milton's remarks on the imitation of the passions would have seemed impeccably Aristotelian. Milton's reference to Aristotle's mimesis at this point could, moreover, serve a rhetorical purpose as well as a doctrinal end. By alluding to the role of imitation in arousing delight, he was indirectly reinforcing his defense of his own practice in following the ancients. The passions may be dangerous if ill imitated (in *The Reason of Church-Government* he censures the moderns for imitating badly and accordingly communicating "vitious principles in sweet pils"), but if "well imitated" they may be truly medicinal. Tragedy can be morally useful only if it arouses the proper delight; it can purge the passions only if it imitates them well. Milton's reference to the delight "stirr'd up" by imitation provides a fuller and more comprehensive explanation of tragic effect. But it also serves as a rhetorical argument to support his apologia for tragedy "as it was antiently compos'd." [27]

FROM THE DELIGHT aroused by imitation (a thoroughly conventional doctrine in neo-Aristotelian poetics) let us turn to the fourth major idea in Milton's *explicatio*, the imitation of the passions. For many twentieth-century critics, this doctrine does *not* seem Aristotelian; and John Arthos, observing that Aristotle had defined tragedy as an "imitation of an action," not of passion, has advanced the interesting but not altogether convincing suggestion that Milton may have derived this "modification of Aristotle" from Italian musical theory. Monteverdi, for instance, "spoke insistently of his work as imitation, and as imitation of the passions." [28]

In actuality, like most of the ideas in Milton's preface, this was a Renaissance commonplace. Although it did not pass unchallenged, it entered neo-Aristotelian criticism virtually at the beginning, in Maggi's lectures on the *Poetics*, [29] and it was reaffirmed

27. Aristotle, *On the Art of Poetry*, ed. and trans. Bywater, 39; Milton, *The Reason of Church-Government*, in *Yale Prose*, I, 818.
28. Arthos, *Milton and the Italian Cities*, 155–86.
29. See Weinberg, *History of Literary Criticism*, I, 534–35, 555, on the views of

by numerous other commentators—Tomitano, Robortello, Lionardi, Tasso, Segni, Piccolomini, Gambara, Varchi, and Zabarella. Other authors, such as Dolce, Lomazzo, Leonardo da Vinci, and the Quattrocento artist Alberti, had adapted the concept of poetry as emotional representation to the arts of design. The painter and sculptor, they argued, must attempt, like the poet, to depict the passions of the mind, albeit by different means. Some of the readers of Milton's preface, moreover, would have encountered this doctrine already—if not in Cinquecento criticism, then surely in Dryden's essay *Of Dramatic Poesy*, published three years before *Samson Agonistes*.[30]

One hardly needs, therefore, to look to Italian musical theory

---

Sassetti and Del Bene. In discussing Sardi's manuscript notes on lectures given by Maggi on Aristotle's *Poetics* at the University of Ferrara, Weinberg observes that the 1546 lectures were "very close in context to the ones that Maggi began giving in 1541; hence by all odds the earliest extant commentary on Aristotle's *Poetics*" (*ibid.*, I, 375). The definition of poetry as an imitation not only of actions but of passions and mores as well appears in Sardi's notes: "imitatio actionum, passionum, et morum" (*ibid.*, I, 380).

30. See Weinberg, *History of Literary Criticism*, I, 22, 206–207, 302, 385, 389, 429, 544, 567, 592; Tasso, "Allegoria della *Gerusalemme Liberata*," in *Prose diverse*, ed. Guasti, I, 301; *Dialogo di Messer Alessandro Lionardi, della inventione poetica* (Venice, 1554), 81; Giovanni Paolo Lomazzo, *A Tracte Containing the Artes of Curious Paintinge Carvinge & Buildinge*, trans. R. H. (Oxford, 1598), 13; Lodovico Dolce, *L'Aretino. Dialogo della Pittura*, ed. D. Ciampoli (Lanciano, 1913), 13; Leon Battista Alberti, *On Painting*, trans. John R. Spencer (rev. ed.; New Haven and London, 1966), 77–79; *The Literary Works of Leonardo da Vinci*, ed. Jean Paul Richter (2nd ed., 2 vols.; London and New York, 1939), I, 38–39, 50, 55, 342. For further discussion of the passions in art, see Anthony Blunt, *Artistic Theory in Italy, 1450–1600* (London and New York, 1968), 12, 34–35, 52–78; Rensselaer W. Lee, *Ut Pictura Poesis: The Humanistic Theory of Painting* (New York, 1967), 22–29, 41, 64–75. Although many of the late Renaissance treatises on painting (or on poetry) claim to base the doctrine of the imitation of the passions on Aristotle's *Poetics*, the relatively early date of Alberti's treatise (which antedated the influence of the *Poetics*) indicates that this doctrine had long been established in the theory of painting. It had, moreover, become conventional in late medieval or early Renaissance poetic theory, largely through the influence of Horace. See John Dryden, *Of Dramatic Poesy and Other Critical Essays*, ed. George Watson (2 vols.; London and New York, 1962), I, 25, for the definition of a play as "a just and lively image of human nature representing its passions and humours, and the changes of fortune to which it is subject, for the delight and instruction of mankind." Again, "imitation of humours and passions" is the soul of poetry (56). The Greek tragic poets attempted to express "the *pathos* of mankind"; and both tragedy and epic depict "human nature, in its actions, passions, and traverses of fortune" (73, 87). Morris Freedman has already raised the question of a possible relationship between Dryden's essay *Of Dramatic Poesy* and Milton's preface to *Samson Agonistes* ("Milton and Dryden on Rhyme," *Huntington Library Quarterly*, XXIV [1961], 337–44).

for the sources of Milton's allusion to "passions well imitated." The doctrine that poetry imitates the passions was already well established in Italian critical theory and had already been introduced, by a major poet and critic, into English criticism. Similarly, it was in all probability to Cinquecento poetics that the musical theorists, like the theorists of the arts of design, were indebted for the doctrine that art is an imitation of the passions.

The theory that poetry represents the passions antedates the Renaissance Aristotle. In various forms, this doctrine appears in classical and medieval rhetoric, in late classical commentaries on Horace and Terence, and in medieval poetic theory. These antecedents, however, lie outside the scope of this essay. Our immediate concern is with the *Poetics*. What justification for this doctrine did Milton's predecessors find in Aristotle's treatise and related works? What verbal authority, if any, did they find for their assertions that poetry imitates the passions?

The principal support for this view was to be found in Aristotle's discussion of choreographic imitation, near the beginning of his treatise. "Rhythm alone," he declares, "without harmony, is the means in the dancer's imitations; for even he, by the rhythms of his attitudes, may present men's characters, as well as what they do and suffer." In this passage the author mentions three distinct objects of imitation—characters, "passions," and actions: μιμοῦνται καὶ ἤθη καὶ πάθη καὶ πράξεις.[31]

The word *pathē* ("passions") is ambiguous, and Aristotle does not always employ it in the same sense. Like its Latin equivalents *passio* and *perturbatio*, it could denote sufferings—the torments inflicted on a man—or alternatively the emotions. In his note on this passage, as in his translation, Bywater interprets it in the former sense.[32] Many Renaissance commentators, on the other hand,

---

31. Aristotle, *On the Art of Poetry*, ed. and trans. Bywater, 2–5.

32. *Ibid.*, 105. Although he observes that the term *pathē* is "generally assumed . . . to denote in this passage 'feelings' or 'emotions,'" Bywater prefers to interpret it in the sense of "what they [the personages represented] have done to them," citing analogous instances of the word elsewhere in the *Poetics*: "The words *pathe kai praxeis* cover the whole ground of the story in the dance; so that Aristotle . . . might have said here, without difference of meaning, *ethe kai mythous*." Bywater also discusses "the variety of senses attaching to" the term *pathos* (204).

preferred the latter meaning. In their *explanatio* on the *Poetics*, Maggi and Lombardi interpret this term as an allusion to the passions: "Per perturbationes autem Aristoteles, iram, furorem, odium, & reliqua eiusmodi intelligit" ("By perturbations Aristotle understands ire, fury, hate, and the rest of such passions"). More significant, however, is the fact that in his "annotations" Maggi specifically attributes the same objects of imitation—characters, passions, and actions—to the poet. He says that all poets imitate characters, perturbations, and actions, but chiefly assume the name inasmuch as they imitate human actions. "Illud etiam adnotandum, poetas omnes, cùm mores, perturbationes, atque actiones imitentur, inde tamen potissimùm nomen sumpsisse, quòd actiones humanas imitentur, ut inferius ex Aristotele constabit." Robortello, Vettori, Piccolomini, and Goulston all interpreted this term as denoting the emotions. The dancer imitated actions, passions, and character.[33]

This, then, is the textual authority for the triad—*mores, perturbationes, actionesque*—so common in Renaissance definitions of poetry and the objects of poetic imitation. Occurring first in Pazzi's translation of the *Poetics*, it was subsequently taken up by Maggi, Robortello, and others, and thus entered the mainstream of the Italian critical tradition. For many critics, Aristotle's definition of tragedy ("imitatio actionis seriae") seemed incomplete in comparison with his earlier remarks on choreographic imitation. If the dancer imitated character and passion, could not the poet imitate them as well? In their commentaries, accordingly, they fre-

---

33. Maggi, *Explanationes*, 50–51; Robortello, *Explicationes* (11 12), bases his commentary on Pazzi's translation ("mores, perturbationes, actionesque imitantur"), explaining that "ratio aut paret, aut imperat, si imperat, parent cupiditates. Si paret, imperant cupiditates. Ex priore habitu, existunt *ethe*. Ex altero existunt *pathe*" ("reason either obeys or commands. If it commands, the appetites obey. If it obeys, the appetites rule. From the former habit results character. From the latter habit results passion"). He also observes that the same triad (*ēthē, pathē, praxeis*) recurs in the *Paedogogus* of Clement of Alexandria, and he further cites Cicero's *Tusculan Questions* on the meaning of *perturbationes*. See Pietro Vettori, *Petri Victorii Commentarii, In Primum Librum Aristotelis de Arte Poetarum* (Florence, 1560), 10 ("imitantur & mores, & affectus, & actiones"); Piccolomini, *Annotationi* (13), dismisses Vettori's doubts and defines imitation as representation of human actions, mores, and passions; Goulston, *Aristotelis de Poetica*, 2 ("imitantur & Mores, & Affectus, & Actiones").

quently broadened Aristotle's definition of tragedy to include the imitation of passion and character in addition to action.

In support of this interpretation, moreover, critics could point to the discussion of music in the *Politics*, where again Aristotle appeared to speak of the imitation of emotion and character: "Rhythm and melody supply imitations of anger and gentleness, and also of courage and temperance, and of all the qualities contrary to these, and of the other qualities of character, which hardly fall short of the actual affections, as we know from our own experience, for in listening to such strains our souls undergo a change." When "men hear imitations, even apart from the rhythms and tunes themselves, their feelings move in sympathy." Or again, "even in mere melodies there is an imitation of character."[34]

Scarcely less important, as a foundation for the view that poetry imitates the passions, were Aristotle's remarks on passion in relation to diction. In constructing his plot and adding appropriate diction, Aristotle declares, the poet ought to place the actual scene before his eyes, to act out his story with "the very gestures of his personages," and to experience personally the emotions he plans to represent: "Given the same natural qualifications, he who feels the emotions [πάθεσίν] to be described will be the most convincing; distress and anger, for instance, are portrayed most truthfully by one who is feeling them at the moment. Hence it is that poetry demands a man with a special gift for it, or else one with a touch of madness in him; the former can easily assume the required mood, and the latter may be actually beside himself with emotion."[35]

Although Maggi suggested that this passage might refer to the actors and the gestures that accompanied their delivery of the words, he saw in it an application of the principle of decorum. He declared the way in which we may appropriately find decorum, which we must observe in figures and gestures. "Dixit modum, quo decorum invenire commodè possimus: cui etiam figuris, ac gestibus opitulari debemus." Robortello emphasizes the principle

34. Aristotle, *Politics*, 1311–12.
35. Aristotle, *On the Art of Poetry*, ed. and trans. Bywater, 49.

of decorum (*tò prépon*) in diction. In order to express the emotions ("animi motiones, ac perturbationes") of individual persons and clothe them in appropriate words, the poet ought to visualize their habits of body, eliciting from these habits the *mores* and speech appropriate to such individuals. As the diction must seem natural (proceeding as it does from men in calamity and agitated by passion), the poet ought himself to feel emotion in order to imitate it correctly. Otherwise, he says, one cannot imitate rightly. For the angry man expresses better the speech and countenance of an angry person. The grieving man the grieving, and the lover the lover. "Alioqui non rectè imitari potest, nam iratus melius irati exprimit sermonem, ac vultum. Dolens dolentis, & amans amantis."[36]

Piccolomini similarly declares that the poet must arouse in himself the same passions (*affetti*), moral states (*costumi*), and qualities that he wishes to portray in his dramatic personages. To depict an irate man he must himself feel anger; to portray a fearful man, he must himself feel fear. Distinguishing three modes of passionate discourse, Piccolomini finds only one that is truly imitative and is capable therefore not only of arousing but also of *expressing* emotion. The first kind of pathetic discourse, by describing atrocities and torments, arouses such horror that it disturbs the delight of imitation. The second kind is Aristotle's pathetic proof; the speaker attempts to arouse emotion not for his audience's instruction or delight but in his own interest. The third mode, however, represents the passion of the speaker and therefore appears to be the natural expression of emotion, when the manner of speaking is conformable to the emotion of the speaker. For nature is accustomed to guide the man in speaking words conformable to the emotions he feels, especially if such emotions are very powerful.

"Quando il parlare tiene convenientia, & conformità con l'affetto, che si truova in colui, che parla, o vuol mostrare, ch' in lui si truovi conciosiacosache solendo la natura guidar l'huomo à mandar fuora le parole conformi agli affetti, che in lui si truovano, &

---

36. Maggi, *Explanationes* (187), observes that several manuscripts contained the phrase *kai holos en hypokrisei*; see Piccolomini's account of Madius' view (*Annotationi*, 245); Robortello, *Explicationes*, 197–98.

massimamente se son molto potenti." Such discourse is imitation, especially if the speaker does not actually feel the emotion he attempts to portray. Like the expression of character (*costumi*), the expression of emotions (*affetti*) is necessary for the poet, but especially, Piccolomini argues, for the writer of comedy or tragedy. The dramatist must impart verisimilitude to his imitation by adapting his language to the emotions he desires to express and imitate ("esprimere, & far' imitando apparire"). Just as the actor imitates by adapting voice and gesture to the words he must deliver, so the poet imitates by making his words conform to the passions of the mind ("affetti dell' animo") and thereby arouses "maraviglioso diletto" in his audience. This third type of passionate discourse seems rather to express than to excite the emotions. This does not so much motivate or excite effects as signify and express the affections. "Non motiva, ò escitativa d'effetti . . . ma più tosto significativa, & espressiva d'affetti, la domandiamo."[37]

Goulston, finally, specifically links this passage with the three objects of imitation mentioned in Aristotle's discussion of choreography: *ēthē*, *pathē*, and *praxeis*. His glosses refer respectively to the imitation of actions ("Sive Res-ipsas oratione imitere") and to the imitation of character and emotion ("Sive Personarum Mores & Adfectus").[38]

IN RECENT SCHOLARSHIP the medical image that concludes Milton's *explicatio* has overshadowed other, and perhaps more fundamental, aspects of his doctrine. In particular, critics have been preoccupied with the problem of sources—citing parallels in Minturno and Guarini—and with the alleged resemblance to modern "pathological" interpretations of catharsis. In his valuable essay on this subject Paul Sellin has called attention to some of the weaknesses of this approach. There are, as he points out, significant differences between Milton's view and those of Minturno and Guarini. Milton's own statements elsewhere in the preface and in his brief translation of Aristotle's definition seem, moreover, to in-

37. Piccolomini, *Annotationi*, 245–48.
38. Goulston, *Aristotelis de Poetica*, 40.

dicate that he held a predominantly "moral" rather than "pathological" conception of catharsis. Finally, in its emphasis on "homeopathic analogy," the "modernistic view of Milton's catharsis" has failed to give adequate attention to "the rest of his remarks on catharsis. . . . Indeed, it would seem that the analogy, rather than the preceding text, is sometimes taken as though it were Milton's explanation of what tragic catharsis is."[39]

As an argument from analogy, the medical image constitutes logical proof. Milton is demonstrating the validity of a relatively obscure poetic doctrine by means of a more familiar medical doctrine. From a purely rhetorical viewpoint, moreover, this analogy bears a double relationship to the preceding passage. It not only demonstrates that like may cure like; it also amplifies the image of "temper[ing]" the passions in an easy transition from the ethical to the physiological meaning of this term. Milton's image emphasizes precisely the interpretation of catharsis that he wanted to stress—not the eradication of the passions, but their reduction to "just measure." Illustrating moral and psychological "tempering" through analogy with the physiological "temperaments" or "complexions" associated with the traditional four humors, he supports his initial statement that tragedy (as anciently composed) is the "moralest and most profitable" form of poetry.

In overstressing the significance of this analogy, scholarship has not only distorted Milton's theory of catharsis (as Sellin justly observes); it has also obscured the rhetorical function of this image. The comparison between poet and physician is far older than Renaissance neo-Aristotelian criticism; almost from the beginning, moreover, it had been closely associated with two principles most frequently invoked in discussions of the ends of poetry—utility and delight. In the *Laws* Plato refers to plays and songs as "charms for the spirit." Since the "spirits of the young cannot bear se-

39. Sellin, "Sources of Milton's Catharsis," in Simmonds (ed.), *Milton Studies*, 108. Warning against mistaking Milton's medical analogy for "Milton's formulation of Aristotle's assertion" concerning purgation, Sellin regards the first sentence in the preface as "a rather careful specification of what Milton thought *ten ton toiouton pathematon katharsin* means. The analogy, however, serves an entirely different purpose: it only bolsters the likelihood that the assertion is true."

riousness, we use the terms *plays* and *songs* and employ our charms as games, just as in treating those who are sick and weak, physicians attempt by using pleasant foods and drinks to give them proper nourishment. . . . In the same way the good lawgiver will persuade . . . the poet to work as he should, and present in his beauteous and well-wrought rhythms and harmonies the gestures and accents of men who are wise, strong, and altogether good." [40]

Proclus inferred from this passage that "poetry should be rather a medicine than a pastime," but Mazzoni interpreted it as advocating "moral instruction flavored with poetic sweetness." Although agreeing with Proclus that "Plato has sometimes called poetics a medicine as that which seeks to render souls healthy, and consequently has the useful as its end," Mazzoni also credits Plato with the opinion that "by means of delight it introduces also the useful." In further support of this view he cites Lucretius' *De Rerum Natura*: "On a dark subject I pen such lucid verses o'erlaying all with the Muses' charm . . . even as physicians when they propose to give nauseous wormwood to children, first smear the rim round the bowl with the sweet yellow juice of honey . . . so I . . . set forth to you our doctrine in sweet-toned Pierian verse and o'erlay it as it were with the pleasant honey of the Muses, if haply by such means I might engage your mind on my verses, till such time as you apprehend all the nature of things and thoroughly feel what use it has." [41]

Lucretius' doctrine, clearly subordinating delight to utility, became Renaissance orthodoxy, along with Horace's precept to mix the *utile* and the *dulce*. Tasso, as we have observed, echoes Lucretius in the opening lines of his epic, and Sidney employs a similar image in his *Apologie for Poetrie*: "Our Poet . . . beginneth not with obscure definitions . . . but hee commeth to you with words sent [*sic*] in delightful proportion. . . . And, pretending no more, doeth intende the winning of the mind from wickedness to vertue: even as the childe is often brought to take most wholsome things by hiding them in such other as have a pleasant tast: which,

40. Gilbert (ed.), *Literary Criticism*, 57.
41. *Ibid.*, 379–80; Lucretius, *On the Nature of Things*, trans. H. A. J. Munro, in Whitney J. Oates (ed.), *The Stoic and Epicurean Philosophers* (New York, 1940), 137.

if one should beginne to tell them the nature of *Aloes* or *Rubarb* they should receive, woulde sooner take their Phisick at their eares then at their mouth." Beni similarly compares the poet to the physician. In a passage that reveals the influence of both Lucretius and Horace, he declares that poetry mixes the precepts of life with pleasure, "tempering with sweetness the bitterness of a medicine." Puttenham alludes to the poet's ability "to play also the Phisitian, and not onely by applying a medicine to the ordinary sicknes of mankind, but by making the very greef it selfe (in part) cure of the disease."[42]

Gosson, on the other hand, converts the medical analogy into a weapon against the poets: "Where honie and gall are mixt, it will be hard to sever the one from the other. The deceitfull phisition geveth sweete syrroppes to make his poyson goe downe the smoother." Milton similarly turns the same image against his contemporaries, "libidinous and ignorant Poetasters" who violate decorum and "doe for the most part lap up vitious principles in sweet pils to be swallow'd down, and make the tast of vertuous documents harsh and sowr."[43]

In its traditional forms, this parallel between poetry and medicine usually referred to the wholesome but harsh doctrine disguised by verse or fable and made palatable by delight. It did not as a rule involve catharsis. Once the impact of the *Poetics* had begun to be felt, however, it was only natural that the medical analogy should be extended to include tragic delight and tragic purgation. Not only had Aristotle apparently introduced the medical parallel into his discussion of catharsis in the *Rhetoric*, but catharsis was itself already a familiar medical term. Scientific and poetic interpretations stood side by side in Renaissance dictionaries; and, as Sherman Hawkins has clearly demonstrated, these medical senses of catharsis were widely known in seventeenth-century England.[44]

---

42. Sidney and Puttenham quoted in O. B. Hardison, Jr. (ed.), *English Literary Criticism: The Renaissance* (New York, 1963), 117, 172–73; Beni quoted in Weinberg, *History of Literary Criticism*, I, 343.

43. Gosson quoted in Hardison (ed.), *English Literary Criticism*, 87; Milton, *The Reason of Church-Government*, in *Yale Prose*, I, 818.

44. Hawkins addressed the Milton Society of America at its annual meeting in New York on December 27, 1968. His topic was "Catharsis in *Samson Agonistes*." For the

From a rhetorical viewpoint the analogy with homeopathic medicine is essentially a variation of an older, more familiar *topos*— the metaphor of poetry as sugared medicine and of the poet as physician. For neo-Aristotelian critics, the homeopathic variant was useful primarily as an instance of the principle that like purges like; whether they interpreted Aristotle's τοιούτων as "the same" or "similar" or "such like," the analogy could still apply. For some (though not all) of these critics, however, the image still retained its original associations with the *topoi* of delight and utility. In comparing the tragic poet to the physician, Minturno alluded to "the force of the passions charmingly expressed in verses"; similarly, in comparing tragic and medical catharsis, Giacomini emphasized the pleasure that accompanies purgation. Both of these writers may reflect the influence of Aristotle's *Politics*.[45]

Milton's medical image is, then, conventional not only in explanations of Aristotle's tragic theory but also in more generalized discussions of the utility of poetry. It derives additional force from the very ambiguity of the word *catharsis*; of all the multiple senses of this term the medical was probably the most widely known. Finally, this image brought into clearer focus most of the ideas Milton wished specifically to stress—the distinction (as well as the analogy) between the perturbations of the mind and the sufferings of the body; the conception of excess passion as itself a disease, or *morbum animi*; the principle that like purges like; and the moderation of painful emotions by mixing them with pleasure, thereby rendering the images of these very passions delightful through imitation.[46]

published version of this paper, see "Samson's Catharsis," *Milton Studies*, II (1970), 211–30.

45. Minturno quoted in Gilbert (ed.), *Literary Criticism*, 290; Weinberg, *History of Literary Criticism*, states that Giacomini compares tragic purgation to the effect of "medicinal purgatives which drive out certain humors from the body, provided that the purgatives have some natural appropriateness to the humors" (I, 627). See Mueller, "Sixteenth-Century Italian Criticism," 148, for analogies between Milton and Giacomini. Like Aristotle, Minturno employs the medical image not only in close association with the notion of delight but also in connection with the purgative effect of sacred melodies. Giacomini, like Aristotle, alludes to the "lightening" effect associated with purgation and says that it is "accompanied by a feeling of pleasure."

46. Vettori, *Commentarii*, 112 ("perturbationem & quasi morbum animi"). Mueller

IF MILTON'S REMARKS on catharsis have been overstressed, it is partly because they have been taken out of context. Their context (as we have attempted to demonstrate) is essentially rhetorical; and in ignoring their rhetorical function, one runs the risk of distorting them. Even Milton's allusion to Aristotle is, as Sellin points out, "conditional"; it is intended to support his preceding statement that tragedy as anciently composed "hath been ever held the gravest, moralest, and most profitable of all other Poems."[47] Milton introduces his allusion to Aristotle's doctrine obliquely, in order to prove and support a generalization already made. The rhetorical relevance of this subject is secondary rather than primary; and it is significant perhaps that (except for its English and Latin equivalents) the term *catharsis* does not occur in this volume at all. The preface is not a systematic treatise on tragic theory, but an apologia or defense of the genre as anciently composed—and of Milton's practice in following the ancients.

Ex pede Herculem. Perhaps a competent sculptor can reconstruct an entire statue from a single marble foot, but it is dangerous business for the literary scholar. Milton's remarks on tragedy are too fragmentary, and perhaps too oblique, to enable us to deduce a complete and coherent dramatic theory from them. Whether he ever arrived, tacitly, at such a theory is doubtful; and if we may believe his own words, the "best rule to all who endeavour to write Tragedy" was to be found rather in the tragic poets themselves—"*Aeschulus, Sophocles,* and *Euripides* . . . unequall'd yet by any"—than in any systematic treatise on poetics. (In this respect Milton was, it seems, faithful to one of the cardinal principles of Renaissance humanism—the stress on example over and above precept, and the emphasis on close study and imitation of classical authors.)

---

has called attention to Vettori's "use of the medical—if not the homeopathic—analogy" in his use of terms such as *remedy* and *cure* ("Sixteenth-Century Italian Criticism," 145). Arthos notes that the seventeenth-century poet and critic Girolamo Bartolommei likewise "speaks of catharsis in homeopathic and therapeutic terms" and suggests the possibility that Milton may have been influenced by Bartolommei's views (*Milton and the Italian Cities*, 192).

47. Sellin, "Sources of Milton's Catharsis," in Simmonds (ed.), *Milton Studies*, 108–109.

The preface does indeed throw some light on his concept of tragedy, but it is light of one wavelength; it does not include the entire spectrum. This work obviously omits certain highly important aspects of poetic imitation and purgation that receive expression in his other writings. Most of Milton's remarks on poetics, in fact, are strongly conditioned by their rhetorical context. *An Apology for Smectymnuus*, *The Reason of Church-Government*, and the *Second Defence* are polemical treatises; in these works Milton generally introduces his ideas on poetry as a form of ethical proof. In the tractate *Of Education*, poetics receives tantalizingly brief attention. The preface to *Samson Agonistes* is, as he himself declares, an apologia or defense. Even in his verse and prose epistles his remarks on his literary tastes or his literary plans appear to be partly conditioned by his awareness of the personality and interests of the men he is addressing.

His statement on "passions well imitated" obviously does not exhaust his opinions on the objects of tragic imitation. His remarks are selective, and the selection has been made primarily for rhetorical purposes. In defending tragedy on the ground of its utility (as the "moralest" and "most profitable" of all poetic genres), he had the best possible reason for stressing the passions, rather than action or character or thought, as the object of poetic imitation. Expressed in this form, his argument anticipated, and refuted in advance, one of the most common ethical objections raised against tragedy—that it imitates the passions and corrupts character. In *The Republic* Plato had condemned tragedy on this and other grounds, and his verdict had been boisterously echoed by later opponents of the stage. To these charges Aristotle's *Poetics* was widely regarded as the most authoritative—and, in the opinion of many Renaissance critics, the definitive—answer.[48]

Milton does not, of course, summarize the views he is refuting, nor does he mention Plato by name. He was far too competent a rhetorician to cite the very authority whom the enemies of the

48. See Weinberg, *History of Literary Criticism*, I, 281, on Parthenio's opinion that the type of imitation Plato had criticized was "that of the passions"; see Gilbert (ed.), *Literary Criticism*, 314–15, on Castelvetro's view of Aristotle's attempt to refute Plato's criticism of poetry as passionate and hence injurious.

theater generally regarded as one of their strongest supports. It was common rhetorical practice, however, to anticipate an opponent's arguments and thus forestall him by refuting them in advance. Several of Milton's arguments in defense of tragedy could serve, accordingly, as replies to the objections a hostile reader might raise under the shadow of Plato's authority. In particular, his remark on "passions well imitated" could forestall an appeal to Plato's strictures against dramatic imitation of the passions. His medical image, moreover, enabled him to answer Plato with Plato, pitting the poet-physician simile of the *Laws* against the statements in *The Republic*. His allusion to the poet's ability to "temper" and moderate the passions might likewise rebut Plato with one of his own arguments. For in *The Republic* the philosopher had asserted that "a good man, who has the misfortune to lose his son" will indeed feel sorrow; but "though he can not help sorrowing, he will moderate his sorrow." Similarly, Milton's long catalog of rulers who had composed tragedies might constitute a reply to Plato's contention that tragedy would corrupt the future guardians of the state.[49]

In investigating Milton's sources, one should also consider the factor of rhetorical conditioning. Like most rhetoricians, Milton knew the persuasive force of a commonplace and the evidential value of an authority. As yet we have no clear-cut evidence that he took his theory intact from any single author; in certain respects it resembles those of Minturno, Guarini, Giacomini, Bartolommei, Piccolomini, and Heinsius, but on other points it diverges from their views. To isolate the principal ideas in his preface and to trace each of them to its source is unrewarding. Parallels are too numerous, and at best one can merely amplify one's list of ana-

49. *The Works of Plato*, trans. B. Jowett (4 vols. in 1; New York, n.d.), II, 391–92 (*The Republic*, Book X). Among Plato's arguments against dramatic poetry was the charge that the poet prefers the "passionate and fitful temper, which is easily imitated," instead of attempting to please the "rational principle in the soul." Even the "best of us . . . when we listen to a passage of Homer, or one of the tragedians, in which he represents some pitiful hero who is drawing out his sorrows in a long oration, or weeping, and smiting his breast—the best of us . . . delight in giving way to sympathy, and are in raptures at the excellence of the poet who stirs our feelings most" (*Works of Plato*, II, 278, 382, 394).

logues. These may add to one's knowledge of the variegated and complex traditions that underlie Milton's assertions, but they do not as yet enable one to pinpoint his actual sources with any degree of precision.

The principal source of Milton's statements seems, indeed, to be Aristotle himself—though Aristotle as seen and interpreted through Renaissance eyes. Milton's discussion is, it seems, a skillfully composed mosaic of ideas and phrases derived from Aristotle's own writings, from the *Ethics* and *Politics* as well as the *Poetics*. Even his medical analogy, though conventional in Renaissance poetic theory, is in a sense "authorized" by the medical comparison Aristotle had employed near the end of his *Politics*.

On the whole, Milton was nominally faithful to the authority he cited in introducing his short account of purgation. Like many other critics of his period, he utilized Aristotle to explain Aristotle. Much of the opening section of the preface reveals Aristotelian influence either in diction or in doctrine. Most of its principal ideas were, in varying degrees, conventional in Renaissance neo-Aristotelian criticism. All of them had been accepted, by one critic or another, as implicit or explicit in the *Poetics*.

Recent criticism of Milton's preface has, perhaps, placed an exaggerated, if paradoxical, emphasis on both its originality and its orthodoxy. One doubts that Milton would have been flattered by either term. None of the major ideas in the preface was really original; all were derivative, and most were conventional. Novelty and paradox might command an audience's attention, but they were not always the most effective instruments of persuasion. Although they undoubtedly had their place in mock-defense and mock-encomium, the apologist normally appealed to accepted opinions, to acknowledged authorities, and to commonplaces. In the context of Renaissance critical theory, on the other hand, "orthodoxy" is not an altogether valid concept. Cinquecento criticism was, in a sense, constantly in *quest* of poetic orthodoxy (or "right opinion") without ever quite managing to find it. For many Cinquecento critics the norm or standard was the text of the *Poetics* itself, but this was sometimes too ambiguous to serve as a "rule" without extensive commentary. The text had to be explicated and interpreted, and the explicators rarely agreed. One can hardly speak, therefore, of an orthodox interpretation of the *Poetics*—only of a variety of zealous, painstaking, and sometimes opinionated efforts to ascertain what the orthodox tenets really were, what the classic and most widely accepted canons of poetic doctrine actually meant.

5

SUMMA EPITASIS

THE "MIDDLE" AND "END" OF *SAMSON AGONISTES*

THE *querelle des clercs* initiated by Samuel Johnson's complaint that Milton's drama "must be allowed to want a middle" still continues, though its issues have been frequently redefined and emphasis has sometimes shifted from external to internal development—from the pattern of incidents to that of character or thought. Critics have stressed or denied the hero's moral evolution and the developing though incomplete insights on the part of Samson and the Chorus. The hero's spiritual regeneration, strongly affirmed by some commentators and as emphatically contested by others, may or may not be a precondition for the divine impulse that directly leads to the catastrophe of the drama, but it does (in retrospect) lend probability and verisimilitude to Samson's final and climactic *aristeia*. The same divine power that turns his thoughts to "something extraordinary" has, as we perceive, all the while been restoring him from within, reshaping him spiritually as a fit instrument to deliver his own people (a type of the church) and to wreak divine justice on his enemies. The procatarctic or external cause of his triumph—the occasion—has been present in the minds of the principal actors all along, though they have not understood its full or real significance. This is the Dagonalia; and it is the occasion not only for Samson's unaccustomed leisure to

Previously published, in slightly different form, as "Milton's 'Summa Epitasis': The End of the Middle of *Samson Agonistes*," in *Modern Language Review*, LXIX (1974), 730–44. Used with permission.

meditate on his promised destiny and his egregious failure but also for the visits of his sundry friends and enemies. The other principal causes of the catastrophe, which Milton must and does emphasize, are the proegumenic or internal causes—first, the state and quality of Samson's will, for he is the principal *agonistes* in the catastrophe; second, the miraculous nature of his divinely given strength, for this is the instrument whereby he accomplishes his divine mission; and third, the divine impulse—the "rousing motions"—immediately communicated by the Deity himself as assisting cause ("favouring and assisting to the end"). External and internal causes are, in fact, interwoven throughout the drama (though their interconnections are not fully apparent until the close); and, brought definitely together in the catastrophe, they exhibit the logic and coherence of a providential design. In retrospect, character and thought confer probability on the events of the fable, even though the dramatis personae themselves are not fully aware of this connection at the time.[1]

1. Among the studies of *Samson Agonistes*, see William Riley Parker, *Milton's Debt to Greek Tragedy in "Samson Agonistes"* (Baltimore and London, 1937); F. Michael Krouse, *Milton's Samson and the Christian Tradition* (Princeton, 1949); M. E. Grenander, "Samson's Middle: Aristotle and Dr. Johnson," *University of Toronto Quarterly*, XXIV (1955), 377–89; Ann Gossman, "Milton's Samson as the Tragic Hero Purified by Trial," *Journal of English and Germanic Philology*, LXI (1962), 528–41; French Fogle, "The Action of *Samson Agonistes*," in Max F. Schulz (ed.), *Essays in American and English Literature Presented to Bruce Robert McElderry, Jr.* (Athens, Ohio, 1967), 177–91; Arnold Stein, *Heroic Knowledge: An Interpretation of "Paradise Regained" and "Samson Agonistes"* (Minneapolis, 1957); A. S. P. Woodhouse, "Tragic Effect in *Samson Agonistes*," *University of Toronto Quarterly*, XXVIII (1959), 205–22; James Holly Hanford, "*Samson Agonistes* and Milton in Old Age," in his *Studies in Shakespeare, Milton, and Donne* (New York, 1925); Don Cameron Allen, *The Harmonious Vision: Studies in Milton's Poetry* (Baltimore, 1954); Roger B. Wilkenfeld, "Act and Emblem: The Conclusion of *Samson Agonistes*," *ELH*, XXXII (1965), 160–68; G. A. Wilkes, "The Interpretation of *Samson Agonistes*," *Huntington Library Quarterly*, XXVI (1963), 363–79; Paul R. Sellin, "Sources of Milton's Catharsis: A Reconsideration," *Journal of English and Germanic Philology*, LX (1961), 712–30; Martin E. Mueller, "*Pathos* and *Katharsis* in *Samson Agonistes*," *ELH*, XXXI (1964), 156–74; Thomas Kranidas, "Dalila's Role in *Samson Agonistes*," *Studies in English Literature*, VI (1966), 125–37; Anthony Low, "Tragic Pattern in *Samson Agonistes*," *Texas Studies in Language and Literature*, XI (1969), 915–30; Barbara K. Lewalski, "*Samson Agonistes* and the 'Tragedy' of the Apocalypse," *PMLA*, LXXXV (1970), 1050–62; Mason Tung, "*Samson Impatiens*: A Reinterpretation of Milton's *Samson Agonistes*," *Texas Studies in Language and Literature*, IX (1967), 475–92; William V. Nestrick, "*Samson Agonistes* and Trial by Combat," *Studia Neophilologica*, XLIII (1971), 246–51; Stanley Fish, "Question and Answer

Like his admired Euripides, and like Aeschylus and Sophocles
—the "best rule" for tragic composition—Milton must (according to the neo-Aristotelian and neo-Horatian poetics he had inherited) make his tragic event appear probable or necessary by
representing it as the probable or necessary outcome of character
and thought or the probable or necessary consequence of previous
actions. At the same time, the tragic reversal must ideally occur
contrary to expectation. He must make it seem at first glance improbable and unlikely, but (in the close) likely and probable. He
is, in fact, depicting a miracle, and he must make it appear miraculous, enhancing the elements of irony, paradox, and marvel and
ultimately reconciling the probable and the marvelous, the expected and the unexpected, through emphasizing the providential
design underlying the action. Samson's final victory (as the poet
makes clear) is not merely the exploit of a heroic man; it is an act
of God, and Milton has scrupulously delineated the divine efficacy
underlying the tragic yet heroic outcome. He has portrayed the
divinely contrived occasion, which possesses a different significance in the divine strategy from its ostensible meaning for the
Hebrew and Philistine participants in the drama. He has portrayed the effects of the internal renovation by the Spirit in depicting Samson's repentance and faith. He has delineated the divinely
sent madness, or hardening of the heart, which impels the Philistine lords to send for their own destroyer; and he has prepared
for this event by depicting the process of hardening in Dalila.[2] He
has stressed the divine source of Samson's miraculous strength. Fi-

---

in *Samson Agonistes*," *Critical Quarterly*, XI (1969), 237–64; Albert C. Labriola, "Di-
vine Urgency as a Motive for Conduct in *Samson Agonistes*," *Philological Quarterly*, L
(1971), 99–107; P. W. Timberlake, "Milton and Euripides," in Hardin Craig (ed.),
Essays in Dramatic Literature: Parrott Presentation Volume (Princeton, 1935), 315–40.
See also the essays by Albert R. Cirillo, Irene Samuel, Raymond B. Waddington, and
John T. Shawcross in Joseph Anthony Wittreich, Jr. (ed.), *Calm of Mind: Tercentenary
Essays on "Paradise Regained" and "Samson Agonistes" in Honor of John S. Diekhoff*
(Cleveland and London, 1971); and the essays by John S. Hill, Marcia Landy, Nancy Y.
Hoffman, Sherman H. Hawkins, Samuel S. Stollman, and Jackie di Salvo in *Milton
Studies*, II, III, and IV.
   2. See Mary Ann Nevins Radzinowicz, "Eve and Dalila: Renovation and the Hard-
ening of the Heart," in J. A. Mazzeo (ed.), *Reason and Imagination* (New York and Lon-
don, 1962), 155–81.

nally he has introduced the "rousing motions"—the divine impulse—at the crucial moment in the plot. This device recalls the function of the *deus ex machina* in classical drama. Although it is closer to classical practice than to Aristotelian principles of plot construction, it is not only justifiable but desirable on theological grounds; and it reinforces instead of undermining the logical structure of the play.

The "middle" of Milton's tragedy still remains controversial, but the *end* of the middle may conceivably be more easily identified. Milton himself took pains to underline the point of highest tension—the *summa epitasis*—in the choral address immediately following Samson's initial defiance of the Philistine officer: "Consider, *Samson*; matters now are strain'd / Up to the highth, whether to hold or break" (1348–49). The phrase "strain'd / Up to the highth" is a literal translation of a technical term that Milton could have encountered not only in commentaries on Terence but, as Baldwin has observed, in Casparus Stiblinus' edition of Euripides, which Milton possessed and annotated.[3] For Renaissance scholars, the highest epitasis (*summa* or *extrema epitasis*) denoted the point of highest tension or danger immediately preceding the catastrophe of a comedy or tragedy. Lexicographers derived the term *epitasis* from *epiteinein* ("to stretch" or "to strain"), and the

---

3. Milton could have encountered the term *summa* or *extrema epitasis* in Latomus' analysis of Terentian comedy and in Willichius' edition of Terence, as well as in *Euripidis tragoediae quae extant*, ed. Casparus Stiblinus (Geneva, 1602): see T. W. Baldwin, *Shakspere's Five-Act Structure* (Urbana, 1963), 206–27, 238, 298. Latomus regarded the highest epitasis as "the last step before the catastrophe" and in one instance equated it with the greatest peril (*summum periculum*). Stiblinus, in turn, "locates the *summa epitasis* or *extrema epitasis*, for nine plays, always in the fifth act, except once in the second act." Moreover, he usually employs "his favorite term *epitasis* in the dictionary sense of strain as had been conventional from Melanchthon's time" (Baldwin, *Shakspere's Five-Act Structure*, 217, 298). For Milton's knowledge of Terence, see Donald Lemen Clark, *Milton at St. Paul's School* (New York, 1948); Irene Samuel, "Milton on Comedy and Satire," *Huntington Library Quarterly*, XXXV (1972), 107–30. For analysis of the annotations in Milton's copy of *Euripides* and a discussion of their relevance to the Milton canon, see Maurice Kelley and Samuel D. Atkins, "Milton's Annotations of Euripides," *Journal of English and Germanic Philology*, LX (1961), 680–87. See *Euripidis tragoediae*, ed. Stiblinus, 30, 51, 65, 70, 81, 84, 87, 114, 120, 129, 137, 140, 165, 172, 201, and *passim*. Like Milton, the commentators in Stiblinus' volume frequently employed the word *catastrophe*, but did not apparently "use the term *protasis*" (Baldwin, *Shakspere's Five-Act Structure*, 298).

substitute term *intensio* carried the same sense. Milton's lines, accordingly, appear to reflect the etymological interpretation of *summa epitasis* ("highest strain").[4]

This appears to be the point of "highest tension"—though we should not take the words of the Chorus, which have sometimes proved all too fallible, at face value. The tension and the danger are surely greater at the moment of the catastrophe, when Samson is demonstrating his strength in the Philistine theater and Manoa and the chorus of Danites are torn between violent extremes of hope and dread. Nevertheless, the *summa epitasis*, as Milton identifies it, occupies a crucial position in the development and resolution of the plot, immediately following Samson's open defiance of the authority of the Philistine state and immediately preceding the divine impulse that leads directly to the catastrophe.

Milton's allusion to his "highest epitasis" inevitably raises further questions. Where does the epitasis of his drama actually begin—with Manoa's arrival or with Dalila's entrance? Is the epitasis confined principally to the hero's three successive encounters with his Philistine enemies—the fair idolatress, a Siren-Circe figure who finally accepts the role of a Philistine Jaël; the gigantic champion, a Goliath figure and a representative of carnal reliance; and the official representative of the political authority of a tyrannical and unjust state? Are such concepts as epitasis and highest epitasis relevant to the plot structure of *Paradise Lost* and *Paradise Regained*? These questions must await further study. For the moment, let us consider two aspects of the problem—first, Milton's use of the term *epitasis* in his dramatic sketches; and second, the critical terminology he employed in the preface to *Samson Agonistes*. Although these problems are not without relevance for the "middle" of his tragedy, we must defer a more detailed analysis of the epitasis of *Samson Agonistes* for a later study.

4. For *epitasis* or *intensio*, see Baldwin, *Shakspere's Five-Act Structure*, 177–78. For the significance of the term *epitasis* in commentaries on Terence and in the critical works of Scaliger, Jonson, Dryden, and others, see Baldwin, *Shakspere's Five-Act Structure, passim*, and Marvin T. Herrick, *Comic Theory in the Sixteenth Century* (Urbana, 1964), 26–32, 59, 104–10, 119–28, 224, 239. For *summa epitasis* and Scaliger's term *catastasis*, see Baldwin, *Shakspere's Five-Act Structure*, 211, 295, 321; Herrick, *Comic Theory*, 107, 109, 119. See also Bernard Weinberg, *A History of Literary Criticism in the Italian Renaissance* (2 vols.; Chicago, 1961).

MILTON EMPLOYS the dramatic term *epitasis* twice in his notes for tragedies on biblical themes—in the sketches for "Abias Thersaeus" and for "Moabitides or Phineas." In both instances the epitasis is Milton's own invention, and serves to complicate the action and arouse suspense.[5]

The first argument is based on the sickness of Abijah, son of Jeroboam, king of Israel (I Kings 14.1–18). To learn the fate of his son, Jeroboam sends the boy's mother in disguise to the blind prophet Ahijah, who predicts the ruin of Jeroboam's house and his nation for his idolatry. Of the entire family, only Abijah "shall come to the grave, because in him there is found some good thing toward the Lord God of Israel in the house of Jeroboam." Bidding the queen return to her own house, the prophet predicts that "when thy feet enter into the city, the child shall die." Then "Jeroboam's wife arose, and departed, and came to Tirzah: and when she came to the threshold of the door, the child died; And they buried him; and all Israel mourned for him, according to the word of the Lord, which he spake by the hand of his servant Ahijah the prophet."

The biblical narrative is essentially the story of a divine prophecy and its fulfillment, and this provides the argument for Milton's proposed drama. The destruction of Jeroboam and his house (II Chron. 13.1–20) lies outside the scope of the drama; and as Milton's title suggests, he emphasizes the prince's "fearlesnesse of Death." The epitasis occurs only after several preliminary scenes. Abijah is brought onstage and puts "his father in mind" to consult Ahijah. A chorus of elders of Israel bemoans "his vertues bereft them." After much dispute the queen herself is "sent to the profit," who receives the message. At this point the epitasis begins: "the epitasis in that shee hearing the child shall die as she comes home refuses to return thinking thereby to elude the oracle." In the biblical account there is no suggestion to frustrate the divine pre-

5. For an analysis of Milton's plans for a tragedy on the Fall in terms of the three "quantitative parts" of the plot (protasis, epitasis, catastrophe), see Maria Wickert, "Miltons Entwürfe zu einem Drama vom Sündenfall," *Anglia*, LXXIII (1955), 171–206; see also Walther Schork, *Die Dramenpläne Miltons* (Freiburg im Breisgau, 1934); William Riley Parker, "The Trinity Manuscript and Milton's Plans for a Tragedy," *Journal of English and Germanic Philology*, XXXIV (1935), 225–32; James Holly Hanford, *A Milton Handbook* (4th ed.; New York, 1947).

diction. This is Milton's own addition to the story, and it is possible that he may have been influenced by the *Oedipus Rex* of Sophocles. In "Abias Thersaeus," as in *Oedipus Rex* and *Samson Agonistes*, the dramatic action centers on the fulfillment of a divine prophecy. Like Oedipus, Jeroboam's wife hopes to elude the oracle; unlike Jocasta and one of the messengers, she does not (apparently) express distrust in its accuracy.[6]

In "Moabitides" Milton does not describe the earlier action of the drama, but devotes his attention entirely to the epitasis and catastrophe: "The Epitasis . . . may lie in the contention first between the father of Zimri and Eleazer whether he [Phineas] [ought?] to have slain his son without law. next the Embassadors of the Moabites expostulating about Cosby a stranger and a noble woman slain by Phineas. it may be argued about reformation and punishment illegal and as it were by tumult after all arguments drivn home then the word of the lord may be brought acquitting and approving phineas." The argument of this dramatic exemplum of zeal is based on Numbers 25.1–18. Having begun "to commit whoredom with the daughters of Moab" and to worship Baalpeor, the Israelites are threatened with the divine anger. The plague that strikes the idolators is averted from the children of Israel, however, after Phinehas, son of Eleazar and grandson of Aaron the priest, has slain Zimri, the son of a Simeonite prince, and Cozbi, the daughter of a prince of Midian. "And the Lord spake unto Moses, saying, 'Phinehas . . . hath turned my wrath away from the children of Israel, while he was zealous for my sake. . . . Wherefore say, Behold, I give unto him my covenant of peace: And he shall have it, and his seed after him, even the covenant of an everlasting priesthood; because he was zealous for his God, and made an atonement for the children of Israel.'" The catastrophe of Milton's tragedy would have been solidly grounded on Scripture, but the epitasis is Milton's own addition, complicating the plot through violent contentions and raising controversial issues for argument until the dubious debate is decisively settled by divine testimony.

6. See *Complete Prose Works of John Milton* (New Haven and London, 1982), VIII, 556–60.

Both subjects may have attracted Milton for their relevance to the contemporary crisis in the English church and state and their potentialities for antiprelatical and antiroyalist propaganda. The denunciation of royal idolatry by the prophet Ahijah paralleled contemporary Puritan attacks on King Charles's High Church sympathies. Zimri's attachment to a Midianite idolatress of high birth might suggest the relationship between Charles and Henrietta Maria, while Phinehas, who receives the covenant of an "everlasting priesthood" as the reward for his zeal, might serve as an exemplum for the Puritan clergy. Moreover, both of these plot outlines, with their specific references to the epitasis of the tragedy, indicate a concern for structuring the "middle" of the drama. The same concern (one would reasonably expect) would be apparent in the plot of *Samson Agonistes*. In the first of these sketches the action in the epitasis functions primarily as a delaying action or a counterplot; it is designed to prevent the inevitable catastrophe. In the second sketch the epitasis consists primarily in debating the justice or injustice of Phinehas' act, until the issues are resolved, as in the Book of Job, by divine intervention. Both of these features recur in the epitasis of *Samson Agonistes*.

THE CRITICAL terminology that Milton employs in discussing the plot of *Samson Agonistes* derives indirectly or directly from a variety of sources, including Aristotle's *Poetics*, Horace's *Ars Poetica*, and the writings of Evanthius and Donatus. His "intricate or explicit" plot corresponds to Aristotle's distinction between complex and simple plots (Chapter 10). His statement that "it suffices if the whole Drama be found not produc't beyond the fift Act" recalls Horace's remarks on the five-act structure of drama. In declaring that "antient Tragedy use[s] no Prologue," he employs the word *prologue* after the fashion of Evanthius-Donatus rather than according to Aristotle's usage. The prologue spoken by Moses in the draft for a drama entitled "Paradise Lost" likewise seems to reflect "Donatist" rather than Aristotelian usage. The term *economy* for the structure of the plot, which occurs both in the preface to *Samson Agonistes* and in the draft for a drama called "Abram from Morea," also derives from Donatus, as does the term *catastrophe* in "The Argument" to *Samson Agonistes*. His reference to

115

the "disposition" or arrangement of the fable belongs to the terminology of the qualitative parts of rhetoric. Despite their heterogeneous origin, all of these terms were conventional in Renaissance criticism, which had combined Horatian and Aristotelian poetics with the views of Evanthius-Donatus on the structure of comedy with rhetorical theories of the qualitative and quantitative parts of oratory. Milton does not allude in his preface or in his dramatic plans to the Aristotelian terms complication (*desis*) and denouement (*lysis*), *peripeteia*, recognition, or *pathos*, nor does he mention the "Donatist" term *protasis*. Nevertheless, he introduces an oblique allusion to the *summa epitasis*—a Renaissance addition to the "Donatist" term *epitasis*—in the text of *Samson Agonistes*, and he employs (as we have seen) the latter term twice in his dramatic sketches.[7]

Aristotle had distinguished six qualitative parts of tragedy (Chapter 6): "a Fable or Plot, Characters, Diction, Thought, Spectacle and Melody." The "proper construction of the Fable or Plot" is "the first and the most important thing in Tragedy" (Chapter 7); and since tragedy is "an imitation of an action that is complete in itself, as a whole of some magnitude," a well-constructed plot must possess a beginning, middle, and end. The quantitative parts of tragedy are four: prologue, episode, exode, and a choral portion, distinguished into parode and stasimon (Chapter 12). The parts of the tragic plot are three: *peripeteia*, recognition, and suffering (Chapter 11). In a simple plot the "change in the hero's fortunes takes place without Peripety or Discovery"; in a complex plot the change of fortune "involves one or the other, or both" (Chapter 10). Finally, every "tragedy is in part Complication [*desis*] and in part Dénouement [*lysis*]; the incidents before the opening scene, and often certain also of those within the play, forming the Complication; and the rest the Dénouement." By "Complication [Aristotle means] all from the beginning of the

---

7. According to Horace's *Ars Poetica*, "A play which is to be in demand and, after production, to be revived, should consist of five acts—no more, no less" (Allan H. Gilbert [ed.], *Literary Criticism: Plato to Dryden* [rpr. Detroit, 1962], 134). Compare Baldwin, *Shakspere's Five-Act Structure*, 110–13. For *oeconomia*, see *ibid.*, 36, 49, 208, 214, 217; Herrick, *Comic Theory*, 94, 98, 101–106.

story to the point just before the change in the hero's fortunes; by Dénouement, all from the beginning of the change to the end" (Chapter 18).[8]

In analyzing the plot structure of *Samson Agonistes*, scholars have justifiably emphasized the importance of Aristotle's *Poetics* and its Renaissance commentaries. A quotation from this work provides the epigraph for Milton's preface, and in other works he expresses respect for the rules of Aristotle. Nevertheless, we cannot rely on the Aristotelian tradition alone. As the preface and "The Argument" to his drama and his sketches for biblical tragedies indicate, he also thought in the "Donatist" categories that he had probably encountered as a schoolboy in commentaries on Terence and subsequently in analyses of both Greek and Latin tragedy and in Renaissance neo-Aristotelian poetic theory.

According to *Evanthius De Fabula* and the *De Comoedia* (both associated with Donatus' commentaries on Terence), the quantitative parts of comedy are prologue, protasis, epitasis, and catastrophe. According to Evanthius, the prologue is "a kind of preface to the play, in which alone it is permitted to present to the people matter extraneous to the argument, either on behalf of the poet, the play itself, or the actors," while the other treatise defines prologue either as "the first speech" or a "set speech anteceding the true composition of the play." According to Aristotle, on the other hand, the "Prologue is all that precedes the Parode of the chorus" (Chapter 12). In the preface to *Samson Agonistes*, Milton's use of the word *prologue* is closer to Evanthius' conception of its function (and to the *De Comoedia*'s second definition) than to Aristotle's. By Aristotle's definition, and by the first definition in the *De Comoedia*, Samson's entire first speech (ll. 1–114) would be the prologue. Moses' prologue in the dramatic plan for "Paradise Lost" seems to have been conceived rather as a "set speech anteceding the true composition of the play" than as a prologue in the Aristotelian sense.[9]

Evanthius defines the protasis as "the first act, and beginning of

8. *Aristotle on the Art of Poetry*, trans. Ingram Bywater (Oxford, 1945), 36, 39–40, 48, 46, 63.
9. Baldwin, *Shakspere's Five-Act Structure*, 33; *Aristotle on the Art of Poetry*, trans.

the drama," and the *De Comoedia* similarly identifies it as "the first act of the play, in which part of the argument is unfolded, part concealed so as to hold the expectation of the audience." The epitasis is the "increase and progression of the turbations, and the whole . . . knot of the error" (Evanthius), and "the involution of the argument, by the elegance of which it is knotted together" (*De Comoedia*). Finally, the catastrophe is "the conversion of affairs into a happy ending" (Evanthius), and "the solution of the play, through which its outcome is made good" (*De Comoedia*).[10]

The influence of this scheme of classification on Renaissance interpretations of classical comedy and tragedy and on Neo-Latin and vernacular drama has been examined in detail by T. W. Baldwin and by Marvin T. Herrick—the former primarily in terms of its significance for Shakespeare's five-act structure; the latter, in terms of sixteenth-century comic theory. Since Milton did not divide his poem into act and scene (since it "never was intended" for the stage), observing merely that it does not extend beyond the fifth act, we shall not consider questions of act division. Instead, we shall concentrate on the significance of the Evanthius-Donatus conception of epitasis for the long-lost middle of *Samson Agonistes*.

In the first place, the epitasis was associated with the knot of error, with perturbation and tumult frequently resulting from error, and with perils.[11] A late fifteenth-century editor of Seneca

---

Bywater, 48; compare the introductory monologues (or prologues) in Milton's sketch for "Adam Unparadized" and in *Comus*.

10. Baldwin, *Shakspere's Five-Act Structure*, 33.

11. *Ibid.*, 43–44. See also 235 for Willichius' description of the epitasis and catastrophe of tragedy: "In the epitasis [are] great fears, contentions, crafty fetches, universal slaughters, and therefore it is called the dissolver [*solutrix*] of life. The catastrophe is utterly calamitous and here all the turbulences are at the height, and *pathe*, that is, the fiercer passions, dominate." In Baldwin's opinion (211), Latomus uses the terms *protasis*, *epitasis*, and *catastrophe* not merely as "points as in Melanchthon," but in a double sense, as "both sections and points within the sections." Moreover, "the peril in each thread of the play has a beginning, which he calls an *initium epitaseos* or *initium ad epitasin*." Compare Robert Stephanus, "Epitasis, turba fervidissima," "vehementissimus actus, qui catastrophen praecedit, in quo omnia quasi fervent et aestuant inter spem et metum" ("Epitasis, very fervid disturbance," "very vehement action, which precedes the catastrophe and in which all things rage between hope and fear"); Ascham, "*in Epitasi*: whan the Tragedie is hiest and hotest"; Kyffin, "*Intention* or *Full Sway*, conteyning the growing on and continuance of all the hot sturre, trouble and difficult state of the Comoedie" (all quoted in Baldwin, *Shakspere's Five-Act Structure*, 314–15, 316, 318).

(Danielis Gaietanus) apparently thought of the epitasis "as the beginning of the perturbations, and the catastrophe" as in the beginning of Hercules' madness in *Hercules Furens*, but also seemed to
regard the epitasis as "the place where difficulties arise because of
the entrance of certain characters." Melanchthon spoke frequently
of the "epitasis of the peril" in Terentian comedy. Melanchthon
"thinks of the protasis, epitasis, and catastrophe of the peril of
each thread of the story. He seeks the wrong which gives rise to
the peril of the chief character in each thread of the story. This
wrong is the protasis of the peril. He next looks for the crucial
point when the character is about to be overwhelmed with the
peril, the point of 'intensio.' This is the epitasis of the peril.
Finally, he looks for the place where the character is released
from peril. This is the catastrophe of the peril." Barlandus, citing
Donatus as his authority, defines the protasis as the "first tumult,"
the epitasis as "the most fervid turbulence," and the catastrophe as
"the sudden reversal of affairs." [12]

In Omphalius' analysis of Plautus, Baldwin finds a conception
of the peril, as "the place where the peril becomes fully formed
and crucial," similar to Melanchthon's definition of epitasis. In
Omphalius' scheme, the three inner acts of a drama "work up to a
crucial scene or scenes of peril," with the peril generally placed in
the fourth act, and finally to the catastrophe. Minturno identifies
the major divisions of tragedy as protasis, "which being . . . the
proposition of affairs explains part of the play, prepares the peril";
epitasis, "where the action, being developed, is thrown into perturbation, or increases the peril, or brings on some evil"; and catastrophe, "where as if by the conversion of affairs, the outcome of
the argument is unfolded, whether the fortune is changed for the
better, or as almost always happens, for the worse." [13]

Second, Aristotle's "triple division of beginning, middle, and

---

12. Danielis Gaietanus, Melanchthon, and Barlandus all quoted in *ibid.*, 151–52,
182–83, 187, 190.
13. Omphalius and Minturno quoted in *ibid.*, 197, 291. For epitasis as *periculum*,
see 182–88, 193, and as *vehementia*, see 177. For epitasis and *perturbatio*, see 39, 44,
49, 202, 204, 224, 233, 238, 240, 256, 263. Compare *peril* in Latomus' analysis of
Terence, 209, 216–17.

119

end is cognate with the protasis, epitasis, and catastrophe as in Donatus"; the epitasis of a comic plot could correspond to the middle of a tragic fable. This correlation was further accentuated by the tendency to identify the Donatist epitasis with the Aristotelian episode. Aristotle had defined "an Episode [as] all that comes between two whole choral songs" (Chapter 12). As Baldwin has shown, Renaissance theorists inherited through Tzetzes a fourfold classification of the parts of comedy ultimately based on Aristotle's discussion of tragedy (prologue, choric ode, episode, exode) and equated them with the Donatist fourfold division. Epitasis would therefore correspond to episode.[14]

Camerarius recommended applying the Donatist distinctions (protasis, or "beginning"; epitasis, or "increment"; and catastrophe, or "end") to tragedy "for the purpose of teaching," and defined episode as "whatever is inserted, the argument not requiring it." As Baldwin observes, Camerarius perceived no fundamental "conflict on structure" in the systems of Aristotle and Donatus. Although later commentators disagreed as to whether "there was only one episode, or three," they usually agreed that "the term corresponded to the term epitasis in Donatus."[15]

Third, as Baldwin has shown, Melanchthon and other Renaissance scholars frequently interpreted the Evanthius-Donatus terminology in light of lexicographical definitions, defining *prothesis* (or *protasis*) as proposition, *epitasis* as *intensio* (literally, "stretching"), and catastrophe as *conversio* (or *subversio* or *devastatio*). An

14. *Ibid.*, 53, 62; *Aristotle on the Art of Poetry*, trans. Bywater, 48–49; Baldwin, *Shakspere's Five-Act Structure*, 107–108, 144, 154.

15. Baldwin, *Shakspere's Five-Act Structure*, 198; see also 200–202 for Camerarius' use of the term *epitasis* in his analysis of the tragedies of Sophocles. According to Baldwin, Camerarius regarded the epitasis both as "a section, the place of the turbations" and as a "particular point of points, the places of tension or highest turbation" (204). For epitasis and episode in Italian theories of tragic construction and neo-Aristotelian poetic theory, see 253, 255–56, 265, 271–73, 278–79, 285–306. Compare Pigna on episode as epitasis, and Piccolomini on the three episodes in tragedy; Riccoboni regards the second, third, and fourth acts as episode (294, 299, 303–305). This "triplex episode" constitutes the epitasis or else consists of two parts, epitasis and catastasis. Castelvetro argues that the Aristotelian episode "is divided into three, and there are three episodes" corresponding to the second, third, and fourth acts. The parts of a tragedy are "prologue, entering chorus, episode, stationary chorus, episode, stationary chorus, episode, stationary chorus, exode" (289–99).

alternative designation for the point of highest tension immediately preceding the catastrophe was Scaliger's term *catastasis*.
Both Herrick and Baldwin regard this as the equivalent of the
summa epitasis of a play. In these commentaries, the catastrophe
frequently corresponds to the Aristotelian *peripeteia*, or reversal,
and *lysis*, or denouement; the Aristotelian *desis*, or complication,
apparently comprises the preceding parts of the fable (protasis,
epitasis, and highest epitasis or catastasis).[16]

In addition to the critical distinctions between protasis, epitasis,
and catastrophe, Milton would have encountered other concepts
in these commentaries which might prove useful in his dramatic
plans and in the construction of *Samson Agonistes*. The commentators frequently emphasize the poet's preparation (*parasceve*) for
the entrance of a character, for the errors and perils of future
scenes, and for the catastrophe itself; his representation of the occasions for both major and minor events; the complaints and
laments of the characters; shifts in expectation and alternation
between hope and fear or despair; and the use of a *persona ad catastropham machinata* as an alternative to a *deus ex machina*. In several instances, moreover, they employ medical imagery, comparing
the turmoils of the epitasis to a disease and comparing the solution to a medicinal remedy.[17]

16. Baldwin, *Shakspere's Five-Act Structure*, 177–78, 193, 323; Herrick, *Comic Theory*, 119–20. See Scaliger on epitasis, "in which turbulences are either begun or made
tense," and catastasis ("the full vigor and crisis of the play, in which the intrigue is
embroiled in that tempest of chance, into which it has been drawn"), in Baldwin,
Shakspere's Five-Act Structure, 295. Correa associates the epitasis with the place "where
the turmoils are planned, and either begun or made tense" and regards the catastasis
as "the crisis of the play, in which the intrigue is embroiled" (306). For Godwyn, the
epitasis is "the intension or exaggeration of matters," while the catastasis is "the state
and full vigour of the play" (321). Dryden identifies the epitasis with the "working up of
the plot; where the play grows warmer, the design or action of it is drawing on, and you
see something promising that it will come to pass"; on the other hand, the catastasis is
the "counterturn, which destroys that expectation, imbroils the action in new difficulties, and leaves you far distant from that hope in which it found you" (323). The
medical associations of the dramatic terms *status* ("state"), which may signify the crisis
of a disease (312–13, 322–23), are especially interesting in view of the medical imagery
of Milton's *Samson Agonistes* and the prominence of the theme of disease in his sketch for
a drama on Abijah.

17. For preparation (*parasceve*), see Baldwin, *Shakspere's Five-Act Structure*, 47, 184,
186, 192, 207–208, 215, 219–20, 323, 341, 386, 396; for occasions, 181, 183, 196,

121

LEAVING ASIDE the question of act and scene division, let us attempt to distinguish the principal divisions of Milton's plot according to the several alternative classifications current in Renaissance dramatic analysis. The complication (*desis*) would include the entire drama up to the catastrophe; both protasis and epitasis according to the Evanthius-Donatus terminology; prologos, parodos, and all five episodes and stasima, according to Parker's Aristotelian analysis. The denouement, in turn, would constitute the final portion of the drama—the exodos in Parker's analysis, the catastrophe in "Donatist" terms. This section would include the *peripeteia*, or reversal (frequently identified with the catastrophe or *conversio*), and also the *pathos*, or scene of suffering, if one accepts Mueller's suggestion for the position of the *pathos* in this play. There is no prologue in the sense that Evanthius employs this term; nevertheless, Samson's initial monologue is a true prologue by Aristotle's definition.[18]

Within these divisions classification is more difficult. Milton explicitly identifies his *summa epitasis*, but he does not specify the actual beginning of the epitasis; this could be either the scene with Manoa or the scene with Dalila. Second, Milton does not employ the term *protasis*, and Baldwin finds no references to this term in Stiblinus' annotations on Euripides. Stiblinus refers on several occasions to the prologue, employing this word in the Aristotelian sense, as the initial speech in a tragedy preceding the parados. The *De Comoedia* associated with Donatus defines prologue not only as a prefatory speech preceding the drama but alternatively as the first speech within the play. The latter definition could fit the prologues of the plays of Euripides, as well as the prologos of Milton's *Samson Agonistes*. In this case the exact beginning of the protasis in a Greek tragedy might seem dubious: did it begin with the

211–15, 219, 224–25, 241, 277, 284–85, 292; for complaints and laments, 208, 214–15; for shifts in expectation and alternation between hope and fear or despair, 34, 117, 158, 247, 315, 323; for the *persona ad catastropham machinata* and for *deus ex machina*, 40, 56, 58, 61–62, 111; for the imagery of disease and remedy, 158, 312, 322–23.

    18. Parker, *Milton's Debt to Greek Tragedy*, 30–54; Mueller, "*Pathos* and *Katharsis*," 156–74.

prologus or with the parodos? The fact that earlier critics had equated the Greek prologue and choral song with the prologue and protasis of Evanthius-Donatus and applied them to comedy and tragedy alike would further complicate the problem of significant terminology. Since Milton does not use the term *protasis*, it would be wiser to refrain from imposing this term on the first part of his drama.

MILTON SENSIBLY refrained from dividing *Samson Agonistes* into acts and scenes. In the Trinity manuscript he provides a five-act structure for "Paradise Lost"; but in his other dramatic sketches he does not indicate act divisions, though he does at times describe the functions of the chorus. Renaissance critics disagreed as to whether Greek tragedy should be divided into acts, and it is possible that Milton himself had not made up his mind on this point. When he declares "that *Chorus* is here introduc'd after the Greek manner, not antient only but modern, and still in use among the *Italians*," he is probably alluding not to the later Italian dramatists who preferred the Senecan model and tended to confine the chorus to a final song at the end of each act, but to the earlier Italian writers (like Trissino, Rucellai, Martelli, and Pazzi) whose tragedies were based on Greek models. Even though Stiblinus' edition and other Renaissance translations (such as Dolce's versions of *Hecuba* and *Jocasta*) had divided the tragedies of Euripides into five acts for the convenience of the reader, the surviving texts of the Greek tragic dramatists were undivided, as Milton must have known; in refusing to specify act divisions, he was following classical precedent.[19]

Although various attempts have been made to impose a five-act structure on *Samson Agonistes*, none has proved completely satisfactory, and in Parker's opinion we should "be wise, perhaps, to follow Milton's suggestion and ignore the problem." Parker's own analysis of the play's structure is based on the terminology of Aristotle's *Poetics* (Chapter 12), dividing the poem into prologos, parodos, five episodes and stasima, the exodos and a *kommos*.

19. Baldwin, *Shakspere's Five-Act Structure*, 197–206, 276–78, 296–98.

Hanford finds this analysis consistent with a five-act structure, but it would actually result in a seven-act structure according to the system of analysis employed by many Renaissance critics. Although they differed in their interpretations, many of them regarded Aristotle's episode (the epitasis of the drama) as composed of three episodes corresponding to the second, third, and fourth acts. The portions preceding the episodes constituted the protasis and corresponded to the first act. The final portion of the drama, following the third episode and third stasimon, constituted the exodos or catastrophe, and corresponded to the fifth and final act. According to this scheme, Parker's identification of the exodos (ll. 1441–758) and Hanford's designation of the fifth act would be correct; this entire section would constitute the exodos or catastrophe of the tragedy. On the other hand, their analyses of the early and middle sections of the tragedy would present difficulties; and these cannot easily be resolved. Parker's analysis results in a seven-act structure; Hanford achieves a five-act division only by combining Parker's prologos, parodos, and first episode and stasimon into a single act ("Samson alone and with the Chorus," ll. 1–325) and telescoping Parker's fourth and fifth episodes and stasima into Act IV ("Samson with two instruments of force," ll. 1061–440). On the remaining line divisions they are substantially agreed.[20]

Milton himself has obligingly located his *summa epitasis* for us. It occurs in the scene with the Philistine officer, and (through the hero's prompt obedience to the "rousing motions") it leads directly to the catastrophe. According to the Renaissance scheme

20. Parker, *Milton's Debt to Greek Tragedy*, 14–17; Hanford, *A Milton Handbook*, 285–86; Baldwin, *Shakspere's Five-Act Structure*, 299–304. According to Stiblinus, *Euripidis tragoediae*, the *summa epitasis* of *Orestes* occurs in the fifth act (30). The catastrophe of the *Phoenissae* takes place in Act IV, but there is nevertheless an epitasis in Act V (50–51). The epitasis of the *Medea* belongs to the fifth act (65). In *Hippolytus*, Act III contains the first epitasis, Act IV the second part of the epitasis, and Act V the last epitasis (81–87). The epitasis of *The Suppliants* occurs in the fourth act (120), and Act IV of *Iphigenia in Aulis* contains the preparation for the epitasis (129). In *Iphigenia in Tauris* the preparation for the following epitasis occurs in the second act; Act III contains the first part of the epitasis, and Act IV contains a marvelous *conversio* of all things and a recognition scene (137–42). The *summa epitasis* occurs in the fifth act of *Troades* and *Bacchae* (165, 172).

whose development Baldwin has outlined, this scene would be the final episode of the epitasis—the last of three episodes marked by increasing tension, vehemence, and peril—and would correspond to the fourth act. Since Samson's external perils do not really begin until the appearance of his enemies, the first episode in the epitasis would apparently be the blandishments of Dalila, and the second the menaces of the Philistine champion Harapha. These would correspond, respectively, to the second and third acts. In this case the protasis of the drama, with its exposition of Samson's situation, the occasion of the Dagonalia, and Manoa's plan to secure his son's liberty, would occupy the first 709 lines and correspond to the first act. This would be excessively long, however—over a third of the entire drama. Alternatively, one could regard Manoa's scene as the first episode in the epitasis, but this would still leave the problem of five-act structure unsolved. It seems impossible to reduce Milton's plot to the three-episode pattern without telescoping two episodes (as Hanford has done) and overlooking the episodic character of the scene with Manoa.

Milton's tragedy will not, apparently, fit the three-episode, five-act scheme of the Renaissance critics, which was based on a misinterpretation of Aristotle as well as a misunderstanding of Greek tragedy. Attempts to impose the categories inherited from Evanthius and Donatus on the Aristotelian plot and on the Greek dramatists could only result in distortion, and Milton wisely accepted the great tragedies themselves, rather than classical theorists and Renaissance exegetes, as the "best rule" to follow in the composition of tragedy. Parker's summary of the structure of *Samson Agonistes* still seems the most satisfactory analysis that has been advanced thus far. One's only variation would be to suggest the possibility of a *kommos*, "a lamentation sung by chorus and actor in concert," in Samson's lament (ll. 606–51) and perhaps in the preceding lines (541–605).[21]

There are, in fact, five choral odes between the parodos and the exodos—"Just are the ways of God" (ll. 293–325); "Many are the sayings of the wise" (ll. 652–709); "It is not vertue, wisdom,

---

21. *Aristotle on the Art of Poetry*, trans. Bywater, 49.

valour, wit" (ll. 1010–60); "Oh how comely it is and how reviving" (ll. 1268–99); and "Go, and the Holy One" (ll. 1427–40). These appear to make Parker's division into five episodes and five stasima inescapable. They cannot apparently be reconciled with Renaissance theories of five-act structure, however, and we should probably forgo the attempt to force Milton's drama into this Procrustean framework.

The techniques whereby Milton links his scenes together or prepares for the catastrophe were conventional in classical drama. The unfulfilled promise, the mixture of true and false expectations, the ironic foreshadowings, the "irony of alternatives,"[22] the religious festival that shadows the entire dramatic action and provides the occasion for the tragic catastrophe—these were familiar devices and motifs in Greek tragedy; and Milton exploits some of them in his dramatic sketches as well as in *Samson Agonistes*. Renaissance commentators on classical comedy and tragedy had noted instances of *parasceve* or *preparatio* in the "economy" or disposition of the plot, linking the scenes together and anticipating later events. Besides enhancing the unity and coherence of the play and the probability of the action imitated, such devices gave greater dramatic efficacy to the imminent catastrophe, the end toward which action and counteraction are inevitably (though perhaps unconsciously) moving. We in the audience can hear the distant roar of the waterfall, and are aware of the fatal current, long before the drifters in the boat are aware that they are drifting, or where they are drifting.

In Renaissance commentaries on Terence, Milton would have encountered extensive discussions of *parasceve*; and in Stiblinus' edition of Euripides he would have found references to *preparatio* that could be relevant not only to the passages of exposition in his prologue but to the foreshadowing of future events throughout his drama. According to the commentary in this volume, the prologue of the *Medea* (Act I) contained the *occasio* of the entire fable. In the first act of *Hippolytus* the prologue created expectation

22. See Anthony Low, "Action and Suffering: *Samson Agonistes* and the Irony of Alternatives," *PMLA*, LXXXIV (1969), 514–19.

of future perturbations and epitases. The prologue to *Alcestis* stated the argument and occasion of the drama. The prologue to *Andromache* expounded the occasion and causes of future evils. The second act of *The Suppliants* contained the *prestructio* for the following epitases. The prologues of *Iphigenia in Aulis* and *Bacchae* also served as *parasceve*, giving the occasion and argument for the whole plot. The prologue of *Heraclidae* stated the argument for the drama, and the prologue of *Hercules* served as preparation for future turmoils and for the "cessionem epitaseon."[23]

Milton's anticipatory devices are, on the whole, techniques that classical dramatists had employed and their Renaissance commentators had emphasized. One of the most obvious forms of *parasceve* for the next scene was to allow the character himself to allude to the approach of other persons. This sometimes provided opportunities for dramatic irony. Samson hears the footsteps of the friends who have come to comfort him (ll. 110–14), but suspects that they may be enemies who have come to "afflict me more"; they do, in fact, add to his affliction—but precisely because they are friends rather than enemies. Similarly at the end of successive odes, the Chorus announces the approach of the characters who will intensify Samson's torments in the next scene: old Manoa (ll. 326–29); Dalila (ll. 710–24); Harapha (ll. 1061–73); the Philistine officer (ll. 1300–1307, 1390); Manoa again (ll. 1441–44); the Hebrew messenger (ll. 1539–40). Examples of this rather obvious method of *parasceve* had been noted in Renaissance commentaries on classical drama.

More significant is the exposition of the occasion—the "solemn Feast" that the Philistines are celebrating in honor of Dagon.

23. *Euripidis tragoediae*, ed. Stiblinus, 55, 70, 90, 100, 114, 124, 168, 179, 201. The notes frequently emphasize motifs and devices that can be paralleled in *Samson Agonistes*; although one would be reluctant to regard them as "sources," they may have influenced Milton's own response to the text. They call attention to the tragic *querela* or complaint (5–9, 186, 205, 206) and the lamentation over the present *mutatio rerum* (161), to deliberative oratory (116), to the consolatory oration (206), to the pathetic exordium (208), and to "popular and insidious eloquence" (4). They emphasize moral themes—the inconstancy of Fortune, the various vicissitudes of human affairs, the divine zeal, the nature and power of *honestas*, the ingratitude of men toward their benefactors. They comment on the return of Hercules from hell "praeter spem" (203), and they identify monostrophic passages in *Hecuba* and *Orestes* (90–92, 210–12).

This provides the occasion for Samson's respite from physical labors and for his more grievous labors of the mind. It also constitutes the occasion for the consolatory visit of his friends, his father's enterprise for his deliverance, his wife's promise of physical liberty at the price of moral subjection, the boasts of Harapha, and the threats of the Philistine officer. It also serves as the occasion for Samson's final release from his physical and spiritual anguish and for his conclusive victory over his enemies, in fulfillment of divine prediction and as the instrument of divine wrath, divine power, and divine justice.

Critics who have objected that there is no causal link between the various episodes in Milton's play—that A does not lead to B, and B to C, and so on—are partly correct. The advent of the Chorus does not provide the occasion for Manoa's entrance, nor Manoa's for Dalila's. The same may be said for the visits of Harapha and the Philistine officer. Dalila's visit does not provide the occasion for the giant's appearance, nor does Harapha's discomfiture lead to the hero's command performance. The officer's visit does lead to the catastrophe—but only indirectly, for Samson defies him. The "rousing motions" inspired by Samson's God—not the command of the Philistine lords or the officer's threats—are the immediate impulsive cause of his compliance, and these lead directly to the denouement.

Milton might very easily have structured his plot differently, and that he did not must have been the result of conscious decision rather than of inexperience and of disregard for the principles of plot construction. It would have been comparatively easy to invent motives that would link the separate and apparently unrelated appearances of the three Philistines. A lesser poet might have devised a liaison between the meretrix and the braggart soldier, or prompted one or both to incite the lords to command Samson's presence at the Dagonalia. Such devices, however, would have detracted from the gravity of the drama and diverted attention from Samson's spiritual conflict to the bustle of events. This aspect of Milton's method may (it has been suggested) be due to the influence of the Greek dramas he had chosen as his models, but this explanation hardly goes far enough. In dramas like *Oedipus Rex* and *Bacchae*, the sequence of events is, on the whole, closely knit, and as a rule one episode leads logically to the next. By Aristotelian standards, Milton's fable would barely escape the disadvantages of the episodic plot. That it does escape them is due less to the interconnection of incidents in the development of the action than to the impact of character development in turn on each successive action and on the final catastrophe.

A closely knit nexus of interrelationships among the various characters and events in *Samson Agonistes* (which Milton was quite capable of portraying) might have fostered the illusion of rapid action and heightened suspense, but it would probably have blurred the sharply focused image of Samson's spiritual isolation. Isolated by his own heroic identity, his sense of guilt, and his divine mission, Samson is no less solitary in his dialogue with father and friends than in his confrontations with his enemies—his wife, the Philistine champion, and the vested authority of the Philistine state. He is most, and least, isolated, perhaps, in the final scene in the crowded theater, surrounded by inhuman foes, but with the Holy One of Israel "favouring and assisting to the end." Throughout the drama Samson is a solitary hero, but in the final scene his isolation is comparable to that of other and less bellicose champions of truth against revolted multitudes: the solitude of the one just man in the theater of the world.[24]

The dramatis personae of Milton's drama are defined almost entirely in terms of their relation to Samson, and to Samson's nation and his God. Wife, father, "equals," rival champion, masters they are either friends or enemies, Danites or Philistines, worshippers of Jehovah or Dagon; and they bear no relation to one another except this. Their visits are unrelated, for they themselves are unrelated; and Milton has deliberately made them so. As a result he is able to concentrate on one primary relationship in each scene—a different kind of relationship in each case—bringing into play a different facet of Samson's character. The continuity of development is evident less in the sequence of external incidents

24. See Douglas Bush, "The Isolation of the Renaissance Hero," in Mazzeo (ed.), *Reason and Imagination*, 57–69.

129

than in the succession of moral decisions and emotional crises; and these lead, logically and inevitably though against expectation, to the catastrophe.

Milton's method of plot construction is admirably adapted to the imitation of character and passion—and to action as the result of emotion and moral decision. Samson's moral victories over Dalila, Harapha, and the Philistine officer confer verisimilitude and probability on his final exploit. After his challenge to Harapha and after the "rousing motions" he experiences, his havoc in the theater can seem probable; after the first dialogues with the Chorus and with Manoa such a victory over his enemies would have appeared unlikely, and indeed incredible.

6

"VERSE WITHOUT RIME"

MILTON'S DEBT TO ITALIAN DEFENSES

OF BLANK VERSE

THAT LITERARY HISTORIANS have usually slighted the early Italian apologists for blank verse is regrettable, but hardly surprising. Theory has seemed, with some justification, far less significant than practice, and indeed the outstanding factor in the evolution of unrhymed verse, in Italy as in England, was example rather than doctrine. Thus Trissino's influence on the development of *versi sciolti* was exerted largely through his tragedy rather than his treatise. The *Poetica* was published too late to have much effect on the course of sixteenth-century drama. What opened the eyes of his contemporaries and successors to the possibilities of dramatic blank verse was, accordingly, not so much his explicit doctrine as the precedent set by his *Sofonisba* and by Rucellai's *Rosmunda*. Very little of the unrhymed vernacular poetry published in Italy during this period was accompanied by critical explanation or theoretical vindication. Convention, rather than theory, gave sanction to its employment in a wide variety of genres. Alamanni's *Coltivazione* and Rucellai's *Le Api* utilized blank verse for the long didactic poem partly modeled on Virgil's *Georgics*. Muzio exploited it for the verse treatise modeled on Horace's *Ars Poetica* and for the poetic epistle. In Italian drama—comedy, tragedy, and

Previously published, in slightly different form, as "'Verse Without Rime': Sixteenth-Century Italian Defences of *Versi Sciolti*," in *Italica*, XLI (1964), 384–402. Used with permission.

pastoral—*versi sciolti* soon became conventional. In epic they achieved only a partial success. With such rare exceptions as Trissino's *L'Italia Liberata* early in the century and Tasso's *Il Mondo Creato* toward the end, few original epics were composed in this medium, but it was a familiar characteristic of vernacular translations from classical epics like the *Aeneid*.[1]

The first English examples of blank verse were likewise indebted largely to Italian precedent rather than to theory. Surrey's translations from the *Aeneid* belong to the same tradition as those by Cardinal Hippolito de Medici, Nicolò Liburnio, and others. The blank verse of Gascoigne's *Jocasta* is a carry-over from Dolce's drama. More than a century later, in justifying his own "*English* Heroic Verse without Rime," Milton appealed significantly to the precedent of poets rather than theorists. Instead of citing earlier critical attacks on "the troublesom and modern bondage of Rimeing" (and there were many he might have cited), he preferred to stress the example set by those "*Italian* and *Spanish* Poets of prime note [who had] rejected Rime both in longer and shorter Works." Here again the primary emphasis fell on practice rather than doctrine.[2]

Nevertheless, the sixteenth-century Italian defenses of blank verse merit considerably more attention than they have usually received. As they often embody the views of authors notable for their own *versi sciolti*, they can throw additional light on the qualities Renaissance poets sought in this medium and in the particular end they tried to achieve. Trissino's *Poetica* lends doctrinal support

1. See such blank verse translations as *Il Sesto di Vergilio, tradotto dal S. Stordito Intronato, in lingua Toscana, in versi sciolti da rima* (Venice, 1540); *I sei primi libri dell'Eneide di Vergilio* (Venice, 1541); *L'Opere de Vergilio . . . tradotte in versi sciolti* (Florence, 1556); Annibale Caro, *L'Eneide di Vergilio* (Venice, 1581).

2. F. M. Padelford (ed.), *The Poems of Henry Howard, Earl of Surrey* (rev. ed.), *University of Washington Publications, Language and Literature*, V (October, 1928), 233; Edwin Casady, *Henry Howard, Earl of Surrey* (New York, 1938), 233–38; Herbert Hartman (ed.), *Surrey's Fourth Boke of Virgill* (Purchase, N.Y., 1933), xxii–xxiii; C. T. Prouty, *George Gascoigne* (New York, 1942), 131, 145. For a study of Milton's preface in terms of the "contemporary extended debate between Dryden and Sir Robert Howard . . . involving the comparative merits of blank verse and rhyme," see Morris Freedman, "Milton and Dryden on Rhyme," *Huntington Library Quarterly*, XXIV (1961), 337–44.

to the unrhymed verse of his tragedy *Sofonisba* and his epic *L'Italia Liberata*. Muzio's defense, like much of his other poetry, is couched in *versi sciolti*. Giraldi's critical theory, with its distinction between the propriety of blank verse for comedy and tragedy and its unsuitability for the heroic poem, provides a rational justification for the *versi sciolti* of his dramas and the ottava rima of his *L'Ercole*. As relatively early statements of the ends and potentialities of blank verse, these defenses are of no inconsiderable value for the history of English as well as Italian blank verse.

That Trissino's conception of "verse without rime" should seem at times very close to Milton's is hardly surprising; as heroic poets both were particularly interested in its suitability for the epic. *La Quinta e la Sesta Divisione della Poetica*, published posthumously in 1562, but originally drafted before 1529 and probably revised about 1549, anticipates Milton in attributing the vogue of rhymed verse to medieval barbarism. The ancient Greeks, Trissino declares, invented rhyme, but perceived its defects and abandoned it. Its subsequent popularity was due to the decay of learning during the Middle Ages. If not the actual "Invention of a barbarous Age," as Milton believed, rhyme was at least a foster-child.[3]

In recommending blank verse in the drama, but sanctioning the use of rhyme in the choruses for the sake of "dolcezza" and "vaghezza," Trissino gave utterance to a principle which he had already exemplified in his *Sofonisba* and which many of his successors—Alamanni, Dolce, Giraldi, Tasso, and others—would follow in their own tragedies. A century and a half later the same principle is illustrated to a considerable degree in the choruses of *Samson Agonistes*.[4]

3. Bernard Weinberg, *A History of Literary Criticism in the Italian Renaissance* (2 vols.; Chicago, 1961), II, 750, see Allan H. Gilbert (ed.), *Literary Criticism: Plato to Dryden* (New York, 1940), 212, 214. For analysis of the *Poetica*, see Marvin T. Herrick, "Trissino's *Art of Poetry*," in Richard Hosley (ed.), *Essays on Shakespeare and Elizabethan Drama in Honor of Hardin Craig* (Columbia, Mo., 1962), 15–22. *Tutte le opere di Giovan Giorgio Trissino* (Verona, 1729), 91, 114.

4. See F. T. Prince, *The Italian Element in Milton's Verse* (Oxford, 1954), 145. For the development of Italian dramatic blank verse, see John Spencer Kennard, *The Italian Theatre* (New York, 1932); Ferdinando Neri, *La tragedia italiana del Cinquecento* (Florence, 1904); Pietro Bilancini, *Giambattista Giraldi e la tragedia italiana nel sec. XVI* (Aquila, 1890).

Like other epic poets and theorists of his period, Trissino faced an inevitable decision between two conflicting precedents: classical tradition and the vernacular. Should the heroic poet employ the unrhymed hexameters favored by Homer and Virgil and approved by Horace and Aristotle? Or should he follow the metrical and stanzaic forms conventional in Italian epic since Dante and Boccaccio—hendecasyllabic verse arranged in terza or ottava rima? Like many of his contemporaries, Trissino temporized. In conformity with classical precedent, he rejected rhyme; but, like his own predecessors in the vernacular, he also rejected the classical hexameter in favor of hendecasyllables. His verse is thus essentially a compromise between classical and vernacular traditions— the hendecasyllabic poetry of Dante and Boccaccio, stripped of its rhyme schemes. His intermediate position, however, has left him vulnerable on both flanks, and he feels it necessary to defend himself. Against the ancients he must justify his hendecasyllables; against the moderns, his departure from rhyme. The classical hexameter, he argues, is unsuitable for the Italian tongue, and the most satisfactory meter for narrative verse is the line of eleven syllables. On the other hand, Trissino defends his departure from rhyme by arguing that the verse forms of Dante, Boccaccio, and their successors are inappropriate for an extended narrative. In a "materia continuata" like Trissino's own subject—Italy's liberation from the Goths—rhyme would tend to check the flow of the verse by breaking it up into minor fragments (couplets, tercets, quatrains, or octaves) and would disrupt the continuity of matter, sense, and construction.

Trissino's denial that rhyme is suitable for a continuous narrative finds a later parallel in Milton's view that rhyme is "no necessary Adjunct or true Ornament of Poem or good Verse, in longer Works especially." His belief that *versi sciolti* lend themselves more readily to the "concatenation of senses and constructions" emphasizes the same quality of blank verse already stressed by Vellutello ("the continuation of the thoughts from one verse into another") and subsequently accentuated by Milton ("the sense variously drawn out from one Verse into another").

In defending his breach with the vernacular tradition, Trissino argues that the stanzaic forms employed by previous Italian poets are not a binding precedent, for they are based on early and relatively imperfect attempts to follow classical precedent. Dante and Boccaccio, writing in the dawn of Italian literature, were handicapped by the shortcomings of the vernacular tradition. Dante was actually the first to write "cose lunghe, e continuate in rima," for the only Italian poetry extant at the time consisted of short, rhymed poems such as sonnets, ballades, and *canzoni*. In employing the terza rima, he was actually attempting (albeit imperfectly) to "far verse, che avessero similitudine a lo Eroico." Although Pulci, Boiardo, Ariosto, and others had utilized the ottava rima in "materia d'arme," they were really following the precedent of Boccaccio, who had been the first to treat "cose d'arme" in the Italian tongue.

Because of its freedom from terminal rhyme, blank verse is highly appropriate for all dramatic poems and also suitable for heroic poetry. Like Trissino, Milton was to exploit the literal meaning of *versi sciolti* to stress that essential quality of blank verse. The play on the word *liberty* in his defense of blank verse ("an example set, the first in *English*, of ancient liberty recover'd to Heroic Poem from the troublesom and modern bondage of Rimeing") hinges on the Italian idiom. In the preface to *Sofonisba* Trissino had already extolled the use of blank verse in tragedy on the grounds of its ability to arouse compassion and its utility in speeches and in narrative passages. Studied rhyme is, he argued, essentially incompatible with the natural and spontaneous expression of grief. In justifying the *versi sciolti* of Agostino Ricchi's comedy *I Tre Tiranni*, Vellutello defends blank verse on the grounds of its naturalness. It had been invented by the ancients, he suggests, as the closest approximation to prose. The poet has enhanced the resemblance of his verse to prose by continuing the sense from one verse to another and by avoiding terminating the dialogue at the end of a line, lest he hinder the natural pronunciation so essential for this style.[5]

5. *La Sofonisba, tragedia . . . di Giangiorgio Trissino*, ed. Giulio Antimaco (Milan, 1864), 6; "Alessandro Vellutello ai lettori," in *Comedia di Agostino Ricchi da Lucca intittolada I tre tiranni* (Venice, 1533); see Weinberg, *History of Literary Criticism*, I, 101.

Milton similarly finds "musical delight" in "the sense variously drawn out from one Verse into another" rather than in "the jingling sound of like endings." Nevertheless, his conception of the function and purpose of this feature is quite different from Vellutello's view. For the Italian critic, this continuation of thought from one verse into another is a means of achieving greater naturalness and a greater resemblance to the natural flow of prose. For the English poet, on the other hand, there is no question of an approximation to prose; he is concerned instead with the musical value of his verse. Where Vellutello advocates the use of blank verse for comedy, Milton defends its exploitation in heroic poetry. One commends its naturalness; the other adopts it for a greater degree of complexity and artificiality. In one instance it narrows the gulf between poetry and prose. In the other it accentuates the divergence between common speech and heroic verse.

In Muzio's opinion, blank verse was a suitable medium for a wide variety of subjects and literary genres. He himself exploited it for his didactic verse treatise on literary theory, *Tre libri di Arte Poetica*, and for the shorter poems of his *Tre libri di lettere in rime sciolte*. But primarily he stressed its value in the epic. Like Trissino and Milton, he believed that the relative freedom of these "rime senza rime" made them preferable to rhyme as a vehicle for the heroic poem. They are, he argued, the modern equivalent of the classical hexameter, and they differ from rhyme as a spacious battlefield differs from the narrow lists of a tourney. Instead of terminating the sense at the end of a verse, they preserve continuity of style and permit the meaning to flow freely without the interruptions of rhyme. They are, accordingly, loftier, purer, and more splendid than all other verse forms. The "native liberty" of great subjects demands a verse form equally free. For Muzio, rhyme and blank verse differ in quality as the lyric differs from heroic poetry. The poet who seeks to achieve grace through terminal rhyme confines his thought within the rhyming lines. As blank verse is free from such restrictions, it is preferable for the poet who treats heroic themes. Lofty enterprises require blank verse ("Et è la mia sentenza, che l'imprese Alte, & superbe senza suon di rima Debbian trattarsi"), and in proof of this dictum Muzio quotes several "rime sciolte" which are "honoratamente, & gravemente dette."[6]

To the possible objection that blank verse is too short for noble subjects, Muzio replies that Greek and Latin poets had treated high, low, and intermediate matters in the same verse. If diction, ornament, and spirit are appropriate, one does not need lines of greater length. Muzio also proffers advice to the practitioner of blank verse. The poet must guard against introducing an occasional rhyme. But there is also a practical advantage in the use of *versi sciolti*. It is easier to achieve elevation and smoothness in this medium, as the poet is not tempted to choose a plain or rough word for the sake of his rhyme. Blank verse, Muzio insists, with Trissino and Milton, confers liberty. It frees the poet from the bondage of "binding rhyme to rhyme."

Both Trissino and Muzio argue that *versi sciolti* are the most satisfactory modern equivalent for the classical hexameter. A later theorist, similarly concerned with the relative merits of rhymed and unrhymed verse, takes his point of departure from Aristotle's remarks on the suitability of the hexameter for the epic genre: "Experience has shown that the heroic hexameter is the right metre. Were anyone to write a narrative poem in any other metre or in several metres, the effect would be wrong. . . . So no one has composed a long poem in any metre other than the heroic hexameter." Stressing the empirical factor in aesthetic judgment, Piccolomini maintains that the victory of ottava rima over alternative verse forms is to be attributed to the preferences of the majority of learned men. Although unrhymed hendecasyllables seem especially suitable for the epic and although Dante had employed

---

6. *Rime diverse del Mutio Iustinopolitano* (Venice, 1551), fol. 86. Like Muzio, other sixteenth-century Italian theorists stressed the suitability of blank verse for the heroic poem. Bernardo Tasso complains that rhyme prevents the epic poet from varying the length of his periods at will ("con la clausola or lunga, or breve") and that ottava rima lacks the three essential qualities of heroic verse—"gravità, continuazione, et licentia" (see Camillo Guerrieri Crocetti, *G. B. Giraldi ed il pensiero critico del sec. XVI* [Milan, 1932], 318). Girolamo Ruscelli regards the unrhymed hendecasyllable as the vernacular equivalent of the classical hexameter and the best medium for heroic poetry because of its "nobilissima libertà" and "grandezza" (see Crocetti, *G. B. Giraldi*, 318). Carlo Lenzoni similarly emphasizes the appropriateness of *versi sciolti* in heroic poetry as "being most capable of all gravity and grandeur" (see Prince, *Italian Element*, 110–11).

the terza rima, the ottava rima has prevailed because of its appeal to the majority.[7]

Castelvetro's comment on the same passage in Aristotle provides further insight into what qualities the Renaissance expected from heroic verse. He does not raise the issue of the relative merits of *versi sciolti* and rhyme, but the attributes he requires for heroic verse are strikingly similar to those other theorists had sought in verse without rhyme. Like them, he insists that the movement of heroic verse be unbroken and continuous. Like them, he denies that the conventional ottava rima fulfills this condition. His view tends to reinforce the traditional arguments in favor of blank verse, even though he does not direct his line of reasoning specifically toward this end.

According to Aristotle, heroic verse is "the most sedate and dignified [στασιμώτατον καὶ ὀγχωδέστατον] of all metres and therefore admits of rare words and metaphors more than others." Trissino, as we have seen, echoes this opinion, but regards unrhymed hendecasyllabic verse as the best vernacular equivalent for the classical hexameter. As Castelvetro translates this passage in the *Poetics*, the heroic is the "firmest and most inflated" of all verse forms and dispenses with the movement characteristic of other meters. In heroic verse, as in the iambic and the trochaic tetrameter, Castelvetro explains, there is a close correspondence between the movement of the verse and that of the person who recites it ("conformandosi il muovere, e lo stare del verso col muovere, o con lo stare della persona, che gli adopera"). Whereas the trochaic tetrameter fits the dancer and the iambic suits ordinary conversation, the hexameter is the natural medium for narrative verse. Its stability corresponds to that of the narrator himself, and its magnificence and capacity accord with those of the matter it describes. The fabric or texture of heroic verse, Castelvetro continues, ought to be continuous and unbroken, in order to permit amplification and expansion in style and variety in subject matter. One can find such continuity in Greek and Latin heroic verse, but the ottava

7. Aristotle, *The Poetics*, trans. W. Hamilton Fyfe (London and New York, 1927), 95, 97; *Annotationi di M. Alessandro Piccolomini nel libro della poetica d'Aristotele* (Venice, 1575), 383–84.

rima of the Italian vernacular tradition stemming from Boccaccio falls short of this requirement.[8]

One of the most graceful apologies for blank verse occurs in the opening lines of Rucellai's *Le Api*. While the poet was intending to treat his subject in rhymed verse ("Con alte rime"), a choir of bees appeared to him in a dream and bade him compose his poem in blank verse, as rhyme, like all echoes, was repugnant to them.[9]

In a lecture on Tuscan heroic verse, delivered at the Accademia Fiorentina on December, 1553, Varchi examined the relative merits of terza rima, ottava rima, and blank verse in attempting to answer the question, what is heroic verse in the Tuscan tongue? Just as no one doubts that "the gravest and grandest matter that can be found befits the heroic poem, so all acknowledge that the heroic poem should employ the gravest and grandest kind of verse. Nevertheless many persons doubt and dispute what we should call such verse in our Tuscan language. On this point there are principally three opinions. According to the first view, tercets [or terza rima] are heroic verses in our tongue. The second maintains that stanzas [or ottava rima] correspond to Latin heroic verse. The third holds that *versi sciolti* [or verses without rhyme] are the equivalent of the hexameters [of classical heroic verse]." Although Varchi does not attempt to choose among these diverse views concerning Tuscan heroic verse, he observes that some theorists not only approve of *versi sciolti* (blank verse) but "prefer them to all other kinds of verse, especially in heroic compositions." Praising Muzio's learning, genius, and judgment, he quotes the latter's opinion that "only verse without rhyme can and should be regarded as an equivalent for the hexameter, and that it excels all other verse-forms in sweetness, purity, grace, dignity, and brilliance." He observes the popularity of *versi sciolti* among vernacular translators of classical epics and pastorals and cites the examples of Martelli, Daniello, Piccolomini, Caro, and others.[10]

8. Aristotle, *The Poetics*, 95, 97; Lodovico Castelvetro, *Poetica d'Aristotele vulgarizzata, et sposta* (Basel, 1576), 530.
9. *Le opere di Giovanni Rucellai*, ed. Guido Mazzoni (Bologna, 1887), 3–4.
10. *Opere di Benedetto Varchi* (2 vols.; Trieste, 1859), II, 716–20 (my translation, as are others unless otherwise noted).

Other critics, however, were more skeptical as to the value of blank verse in the epic. As Varchi points out, Trifone Gabrieli "not only censured *versi sciolti*, but denied that they were verses." And despite Giraldi's marked preference for blank verse in the drama, he disapproved its use in the heroic poem. According to his *Discorso intorno al Comporre dei Romanzi*, the very qualities that make it eminently suitable for the theater render it inappropriate for a heroic content. Lacking in grace, sweetness, and "heroic dignity," it does not fit the type of poem "which seeks much grace and sweetness with much dignity. These qualities cannot be found in a kind of verse that bears a greater resemblance to everyday speech than to a composition that demands deliberation and judgment with grandeur." Unrhymed verses are "most suitable for the stage" precisely because they seem "free from deliberation, and appear native to common speech. . . . And (to state my own view) I regard as very mistaken the judgment of those who have transferred these verses from the stage to matters of grandeur. If the latter lack rhyme, they are lacking in all that can make the composition pleasing." Its very closeness to ordinary speech disqualifies blank verse as a suitable medium for heroic material.[11]

In drama, on the other hand, Giraldi recommended the use of hendecasyllabic blank verse because of its resemblance to prose and to conversation. According to his *Discorso intorno al Comporre delle Commedie e delle Tragedie*, comedies should employ blank verse throughout, but tragedies could make a limited use of rhyme, chiefly in the choruses.[12]

These principles are, on the whole, valid not only for Giraldi's tragedies but for Milton's tragedy more than a century later. The choruses of *Samson Agonistes*, like those of Giraldi's dramas, resort to rhyme as an ornament and combine "broken" and "complete" verses ("i rotti con gli intieri").

11. Giraldi, *Discorso intorno al Comporre dei Romanzi*, in *Scritti estetici di Giambattista Giraldi Cintio*, ed. Giulio Antimaco (Milan, 1864), Part 1, pp. 101–106. See Crocetti, *G. B. Giraldi*, 301–33, for a discussion of Giraldi's views on blank verse against the background of contemporary critical theory.

12. Giraldi, *Discorso intorno al Comporre delle Commedie e della Tragedie*, in *Scritti estetici*, ed. Antimaco, Part 2, pp. 49–51 (and see 59–60). Minturno similarly prefers rhymed "canti" for the chorus, but requires that the verses in the prologue and episodes be "nudi, e liberi de' legami di consonanze" (see Neri, *La Tragedia italiana*, 123).

Much of the credit for the popularity of blank verse in sixteenth-century Italian tragedy belongs to the theory and practice of Trissino and Giraldi. But their views did not pass unchallenged. A principal issue in the controversy concerning Speroni's *Canace* was the relative merit of the hendecasyllabic blank verse which Trissino and Giraldi favored and the irregular versification preferred by Speroni himself, with its occasional free rhyme and its combination of pentasyllabic, heptasyllabic, and hendecasyllabic lines. Thus the *Giudicio sopra la tragedia di Canace, et Macareo* censures Speroni for not following the precedent set by Trissino.[13]

On the other hand, the defense of Speroni's tragedy involved an attack on blank verse as a dramatic medium. Thus the *Sommarii e Fragmenti di Lezioni in difesa della Canace recitate nella Accademia degli Elevati in Padova* not only upholds Speroni's use of rhyme but dismisses *versi sciolti* as a comparatively recent invention, without grace or gravity. This insistence on the modernity of blank verse in contrast to the established position of rhyme in the vernacular tradition is, of course, antithetical to Trissino's emphasis on the antiquity of *versi sciolti* as a classical norm and his dismissal of rhyme as a medieval innovation. The *Sommarii*, however, seeks to discredit Trissino by arguing that his blank verse, like that of Rucellai, was little more than a device to conceal his deficiency in rhyming.[14] English defenders of rhyme would subsequently raise the same charges against their opponents—that their preference for blank verse stemmed from their incompetence with rhyme.

For many of these theorists of the sixteenth century, blank verse represented the best possible answer to a specifically Renaissance problem—that of finding modern and vernacular equivalents for classical verse forms. They were, however, divided on the issue of its suitability for different literary genres. Most of them favored its use in the drama, on the grounds of its resemblance to familiar discourse, but they were by no means unanimous in recommending its employment in heroic poetry. For some, its conversational quality rendered it unfit for the dignified and majestic epic. In the

13. [Bartolommeo Cavalcanti], *Giudicio sopra la tragedia di Canace, et Macareo* (Venice, 1566), fol. 31.
14. *Opere di M. Sperone Speroni degli Alvarotti tratte da' MSS. originali* (5 vols.; Venice, 1740), IV, 206–209.

opinion of others, however, this was the most appropriate medium for heroic poetry, as the most satisfactory vernacular equivalent to the classical hexameter and as a more flexible instrument than rhyme. Its freedom from the restraints imposed by rhyme made it appropriate for the length and elevation of the heroic poem, while its ability to preserve the continuity of thought from one verse to another was eminently suitable for the narrative mode. Although their theory was less influential than was actual practice, these apologists for blank verse brought into clearer focus the particular qualities contemporary poets sought to achieve in this medium. In the development of Italian "rime senza rime" and "*English* Heroic Verse without Rime" they played a significant, though not a determinative, role.

APPENDIX

ALLEGORY AND VERISIMILITUDE

THE "IMPOSSIBLE CREDIBLE"

IF "MUCH ADVERSE criticism has been spent on [Milton's] allegorical figures of Sin and Death," the blame lies less with the poet or his critics than with time—with the evolution of poetic theory and its inevitable corollary, the relativity of critical standards. The principles underlying the composition of *Paradise Lost* are by no means identical with those by which the poem has been judged. In the case of much neoclassical criticism, this disparity is particularly significant, as its basic assumptions are often so close to Milton's that one might easily overlook their actual divergence.[1]

Whereas Milton's theory of the epic had been based, in large part, on the critical thought of the Italian Renaissance, the theory of his neoclassical successors bore the hallmark of seventeenth-century France. This fundamental difference is most glaring in the very point of greatest similarity between them—their common acknowledgment of classical authorities. Milton's conception of Horace and Aristotle is strongly influenced by "the Italian commentaries of Castelvetro, Tasso, Mazzoni, and others"; the *Poetics* and *Ars Poetica* are interpreted by Joseph Addison largely in light of "the French critics" and by Samuel Johnson in terms of Le

Previously published, in slightly different form, as "Allegory and Verisimilitude in *Paradise Lost*: The Problem of the 'Impossible Credible.'" Reprinted by permission of the Modern Language Association of America from *PMLA*, LXXVIII (1963), 36–39.

1. James Thorpe (ed.), *Milton Criticism: Selections from Four Centuries* (London, 1956), 141; Walter Raleigh, *Milton* (London, 1900), 237–38.

Bossu. The "Rules of Epic Poetry" which Addison, following "Aristotle's method," applies to *Paradise Lost* are by no means identical with "the rules of Aristotle" as Milton had understood them. They are as dissimilar as the Arno and the Seine.[2]

For the neoclassical critic, the chief objection to the allegory of Sin and Death was its violation of the principle of verisimilitude. Johnson condemned the apparent confusion of the "real" and the "figurative" in this "unskilful allegory"—"one of the greatest faults in the poem." In Addison's opinion, "such Allegories" as "the Actions which [Milton] ascribes to *Sin* and *Death*, and the Picture which he draws of the *Lymbo of Vanity*" lacked "Probability enough for an Epic Poem," nor was there a sufficient "Measure of Probability" in the "several imaginary Persons" of the abyss: "These passages are astonishing, but not credible; the Reader cannot so far impose upon himself as to see a Possibility in them; they are the Description of Dreams and Shadows, not of Things or Persons. . . . In a Word, besides the hidden meaning of an Epic Allegory, the plain literal Sense ought to appear probable. The Story should be such as an ordinary Reader may acquiesce in, whatever natural, moral, or political Truth may be discovered in it by Men of greater Penetration."[3]

Although this apparent breach of the "rules of epic poetry" is no longer a very serious fault in the eyes of the modern critic, it presents nevertheless a peculiar challenge to the student of Milton's poetics. Do these apparent lapses from the principle of verisimilitude represent a conscious violation of those "rules of Aristotle" which had occupied the "musing" of the author of *The Reason of Church-Government*? Are Milton's allegories really inconsistent

2. *The Spectator*, ed. G. Gregory Smith (London, 1951), II, 408, 451. Addison adds, however, that critical judgment requires acquaintance not only "with the *French* and *Italian* Criticks, but also with the Antient and Moderns who have written in either of the learned Languages," and condemns the critical pretension of the writer who merely extracts "a few general Rules . . . out of the *French* Authors" (368–69). Thorpe (ed.), *Milton Criticism*, 72; *Spectator*, II, 294–97, 312–15, 330, 350–52, 385–86, 451, 470.

3. Thorpe (ed.), *Milton Criticism*, 83. In the "main fabrick" of the poem, however, Johnson finds no contradiction between the probable and the marvelous (74–75). *Spectator*, II, 386, 432, 452. Nevertheless, in Addison's opinion, Milton reconciles the probable and the marvelous elsewhere in the poem (408, 451–52).

with "that sublime art which in Aristotle's poetics, in Horace, and the Italian commentaries of Castelvetro, Tasso, Mazzoni, and others, teaches what the laws are of a true epic poem"?[4]

Against the background of Mazzoni's critical theory, the most satisfactory answer seems to be no. Mazzoni had explicitly affirmed the poet's license to describe impossibilities for the sake of their allegorical content. In both of his defenses of Dante's *Commedia* he had argued, with considerable subtlety, that literal impossibilities were justified specifically because they were credible on the allegorical level: "it is permissible for poets to feign things impossible in the literal sense, provided these things contain highest truth in the allegorical sense." As orators could legitimately describe impossibilities in their "apologues and parables" purely because "they are true in the moral sense," the same licenses should be extended to the poet. "Why should it not be permitted to the poet . . . to feign things impossible in the literal sense in order to fashion a beautiful and true allegory? Truly I do not know." Both classical and vernacular literature contained numerous examples of this poetic license. Homer had invented the fable of Briareus and "the fabulous chain of Jove"; Hesiod, the myth of Pandora; Hermes Trismegistus, "the fable of Celius, Saturn, and Jove, concealing under this fable the mysteries of God, Angel, and world-soul." Virgil had described the metamorphosis of Aeneas' ships into nymphs and Polydorus' transformation into a myrtle. Similarly, Ariosto's "fable of the old man . . . in the heaven of the moon" and Dante's old man of Mount Ida are "impossible in the literal sense, but credible in the allegorical."[5]

To justify the imitations of impossibilities on the ground of their allegorical credibility, Mazzoni's *Difesa* employs essentially the same arguments as the *Discorso*, but in much greater detail and with a wider range of classical authorities. Besides a more system-

4. Milton, *Of Education*, in *The Prose Works of John Milton*, ed. J. A. St. John (5 vols.; London, 1883), III, 473–74; see Ida Langdon, *Milton's Theory of Poetry and Fine Art* (New Haven, 1924). John Dennis clearly exaggerates the irregularity of Milton's epic and his alleged resolution "to break thru' the Rules of *Aristotle*" (Thorpe [ed.], *Milton Criticism*, 344–45).

5. *Discorso di Giacopo Mazzoni in Difesa della "Commedia" del Divino Poeta Dante*, ed. Mario Rossi (Castello, 1898), 31–36.

145

atic analysis of the "impossible credible," this second defense places greater emphasis on the element of the marvelous and establishes a firmer theoretical foundation for Mazzoni's thesis in an elaborate discussion of the nature and modes of imitation. After distinguishing the proper subject matter of poetry as "il credibile inquanto maraviglioso," the author subdivides the "credibile maraviglioso," or "impossibile credibile," into six species arising from the alteration and falsification of stories and fables; the alteration and falsification of nature ("cose naturali"); the variety of philosophical opinions; an "allegoria fondata nel senso letterale impossibile"; God's absolute power; and the unity of the fable. After a detailed analysis of the first three species in terms of Aristotle's ten predicaments, Mazzoni treats the fourth species (allegory) in terms of a threefold classification derived from Tzetzes, dividing allegory into contemplative, moral, and practical ("negotiosa") and showing "the impossibility of the literal sense and the truth of the allegorical sense."[6]

In Aristotle's opinion, "impossibilities . . . are justifiable, if they serve the end of poetry itself—if . . . they make the effect of some portion of work more astounding. . . . For the purposes of poetry a convincing impossibility is preferable to an unconvincing possibility."[7] In this passage Mazzoni found general support for his defense of the "impossibile credibile," but no specific authorization of allegory. Such authorization could, however, be found, he argued, in Aristotle's remarks on "the improbabilities in the setting ashore of Ulysses." According to the *Difesa*, these "improbabilities" include not only Odysseus' transportation to Ithaca in his sleep but also the allegory of the Cave of the Nymphs in the harbor at Ithaca—an allegorical symbol of the world:

> In those words, I say, Aristotle has conceded that there is a hidden allegory underlying the incredible literal sense. . . . But, to come to

6. Jacopo Mazzoni, *Della Difesa della Comedia di Dante, Parte Prima* (Cesena, 1587), 416–17, 569, and Introduction, nos. 61, 63–64, 84–85, 96–97. For Mazzoni's elaboration of the Platonic distinction between icastic and fantastic imitation, see 391–417, and Introduction, nos. 16–27.

7. *Aristotle on the Art of Poetry*, trans. Ingram Bywater (Oxford, 1951), 87, 91; compare "A likely impossibility is always preferable to an unconvincing impossibility" (84). See Mazzoni's *Discorso*, 31–37, *Difesa*, 403, Introduction, no. 47.

the explication of Aristotle's words, I say that he understood as the principal impropriety in that passage in Homer the fiction of that cave, incredible in the literal sense, and . . . that when he said that Homer had made that impropriety disappear by introducing other good things he meant that with the beautiful allegory set forth above Homer had completely covered that which appeared unsuitable in the literal sense. In that passage Homer directed his entire intention to the allegorical sense and did not hesitate to say things that are incredible in the literal sense.[8]

In both defenses Mazzoni buttresses his arguments by citing Tzetzes, Plutarch, and Eustathius, but in the *Difesa* he also draws extensively on other sources, notably Proclus and "Heraclides Ponticus" (Heraclitus). Palephatus provides him with further support for his emphasis on the relationship of allegory to the marvelous: "According to the Proem of his book on incredible things, Palephatus had asserted that poets turned real events into other things which were incredible and more marvelous, so that they might arouse wonder and marvel in the readers. He clearly shows that poets endeavor to follow the marvelous in the literal sense, but follow the credible in the allegorical sense." For the sake of the marvelous ("per rendere il suo concetto più maraviglioso"), a poet may legitimately falsify "una cosa naturale, o artificiale," provided he does not violate "le leggi del credibile." In such a case the "credibile maraviglioso, & impossibile" is rather to be sought as an ornament than eschewed as an error: "ch'essi sono più tosto da seguire, che da fuggire, e che forse questi non sono da nomare errori per accidente: ma più tosto bellezze, & ornamenti de' Poemi" ("That these are rather to be sought than avoided, and that they should be regarded not as accidental errors but as beauties and ornaments of poems").[9]

Thus, according to Mazzoni's doctrine, Milton's resort to allegory is not only consistent with the "rules of Aristotle" but actually desirable as a source of the marvelous. Such impossibilities as the account of Sin and Death, the Limbo of Vanity, the personi-

8. *Aristotle on the Art of Poetry*, trans. Bywater, 85; Mazzoni, *Difesa*, 586–91; see Robert L. Montgomery, Jr., "Allegory and the Incredible Fable: The Italian View from Dante to Tasso," *PMLA*, LXXXI (1966), 45–55.
9. Mazzoni, *Difesa*, 563–64.

fied abstractions of "the nethermost Abyss," the "golden Chain" connecting the "pendant World" to heaven, and the "golden Scales," which weigh the "sequel . . . of parting and of fight," acquire credibility through their allegorical truth. Through this exploitation of the "credibile maraviglioso" Milton is able to attain more effectively the end of the poetic art—to delight, to arouse marvel, and to instruct.[10]

Although these fabulous elements are, for the most part, credible as allegorical representations of theological, ethical, or natural truths, they acquire further validity through their resemblance to familiar prototypes in classical and vernacular literature.[11] Mazzoni had defended similar impossibilities in Dante, Petrarch, and Ariosto on the grounds that the "cose impossibili" they described had been actually believed by the ancients or else "per la comune fantasia e per la lor fama, erano nel petto de gli huomini domesticate, e quasi per credibili tenute" ("through the communal imagination and their own renown, they existed in the mind of civilized man, and were deemed almost as credible things"). Among these "cose ch'erano credute da gli antichi, anchora che fossero impossibili" ("beings which were believed in by the ancients, even though they were impossible"), were such mythical creatures as giants, Cyclopes, Sirens, centaurs, and the phoenix. Similarly, Castelvetro had observed that such imaginary creatures as "la Chimera, la Scilla, & simili mostri miracolosi, & famosi . . . hanno il suo essere fondata in su la fama" ("the Chimera, Scylla, and similar miraculous and famous monsters . . . had their being based on

10. In the *Difesa*, 572–74, 591–92, Mazzoni defends Prodicus' personifications of Virtue and Delight and similar abstractions in Prudentius, St. Gregory Nazianzen, and others on the basis of allegory. On the ends of poetry, see *Aristotle on the Art of Poetry*, trans. Bywater, 84, 91; Mazzoni, *Difesa*, 417; *Elizabethan Critical Essays*, ed. G. Gregory Smith (2 vols.; London, 1950), I, 392–93; Lodovico Castelvetro, *Poetica d'Aristotele vulgarizzata, et sposta* (Basel, 1576), 664, 668; J. E. Spingarn, *A History of Literary Criticism in the Renaissance* (New York, 1925).

11. The sources, analogues, and meaning of these passages have received detailed discussion in the annotated editions by Newton, Todd, Verity, Hughes, and others. See Harry F. Robins, "That Unnecessary Shell of Milton's World," in *Studies in Honor of T. W. Baldwin*, ed. Don C. Allen (Urbana, 1958), 211–19; George W. Whiting, *Milton and This Pendant World* (Austin, 1958); John M. Patrick, *Milton's Conception of Sin as Developed in "Paradise Lost"* (Logan, Utah, 1960).

report"). Sin's obvious affinities with such classical prototypes as Scylla and Echidna seem to place her in this category, but her composite nature also links her with those "cose imaginate . . . prese da piu spetie, prendendone una parte da una spetie, & un' altra parte da una altra, come è preso il mostro proposito da Horatio ["imaginary beings . . . taken from several species, deriving one part from one species and another part from another species, like the monster proposed by Horace"], 'Humano capiti cervicem pictor equinam/ Iungere si velit, & varias inducere plumas/ Undique collatis membris, ut turpiter atrum/ Desinat in piscem mulier formosa supernè.'" She also belongs to Castelvetro's category of "cose, le quali sono senza corpo, & sono invisibili, le quali il dipintore rassomiglia, come se havessono corpo, & fossono visibili, percioche egli se le imagina secondo la forma delle corporee, & delle vedevole" ("things which are incorporeal and invisible, which the painter portrays as though they had body and were visible, imaging them according to corporeal and visible form").[12]

Thus the allegorical element in *Paradise Lost*—Sin and Death, the Limbo of Vanity, the celestial scales, the "golden Chain," etc.—found a dual justification in the "Italian commentaries." It was credible not only for its allegorical content but also for its basis in "fame" and "opinion"—for its well-known precedents in Homer, Hesiod, Ariosto, and Fletcher. Milton is, however, conservative in his imitation of impossibilities. Despite their value as a source of the marvelous and their credibility in terms of allegory, "opinion," and poetic precedent, he introduces them chiefly "in

---

12. Mazzoni, *Discorso*, 31; Castelvetro, *Poetica d'Aristotele*, 582. Horace, *De Arte Poetica*, ll. 1–4, is translated in Allan H. Gilbert (ed.), *Literary Criticism: Plato to Dryden* (New York, 1940), 128: "Suppose a painter chose to couple a horse's neck with a human head, and to lay feathers of every hue on limbs gathered here and there, so that a woman, lovely above, foully ended in an ugly fish below." See *Dryden's Essays*, ed. W. H. Hudson (London, 1954), 114–15: "But how are poetical fictions, how are hippocentaurs and chimeras . . . to be imagined? The answer is easy . . . the fiction of some beings which are not in nature . . . has been founded on the conjunction of two natures, which have a real separate being. So hippocentaurs were imaged by joining the natures of a man and horse together . . . as Lucretius tells us. . . . The same reason may also be alleged for chimeras and the rest. And poets may be allowed the like liberty for describing things which really exist not, if they are founded on popular belief."

cose accessorie della [sua] Poesia, non nell' essenziale di essa, ò nella principal parte dell' azzione" ("in accessory elements of his poetry, not in essentials nor in the principal part of the action"). Even in a genre whose proper function was, as Tasso said, "il muover maraviglia," too bold an exploitation of the impossible would tend to undermine poetic faith and thereby weaken the impact of the highest, and truest, source of the marvelous in his epic—God's miraculous creation and preservation of the universe, his expulsion of the rebel angels, and his redemption of man. Milton is as reluctant as Marvell to ruin "The sacred Truths to Fable and old Song."[13]

13. Mazzoni, *Difesa*, 585. The quotation is from Bulgarini, Mazzoni's principal opponent in the Dante controversy; see Michele Barbi, *Della fortuna di Dante nel secolo XVI* (Pisa, 1890); Torquato Tasso, *Prose*, ed. Francesco Flora (Milan and Rome, 1935), 332–33.

SELECTED

BIBLIOGRAPHY

Allen, Don Cameron. *The Harmonious Vision: Studies in Milton's Poetry.* Baltimore, 1954.

Ferry, Anne Davidson. *Milton's Epic Voice: The Narrator in "Paradise Lost."* Cambridge, Mass., 1963.

Fish, Stanley E. *Surprised by Sin: The Reader in "Paradise Lost."* Cambridge, Mass., 1962.

Frye, Northrop. *The Return of Eden: Five Essays on Milton's Epics.* Toronto, 1975.

Frye, Roland Mushat. *Milton's Imagery and the Visual Arts: Iconographical Tradition in the Epic Poems.* Princeton, 1978.

Hunt, Clay. *"Lycidas" and the Italian Critics.* New Haven and London, 1979.

Kates, Judith A. "Revaluation of the Classical Hero in Tasso and Milton." *Comparative Literature,* XXVI (1974), 299–316.

Knott, John R., Jr. *Milton's Pastoral Vision: An Approach to "Paradise Lost."* Chicago, 1971.

Lieb, Michael. *Poetics of the Holy: A Reading of "Paradise Lost."* Chapel Hill, 1981.

Madsen, William G. *From Shadowy Types to Truth: Studies in Milton's Symbolism.* New Haven, 1968.

Martz, Louis L. *Poet of Exile: A Study of Milton's Poetry.* New Haven, 1980.

Patrick, J. Max, and Roger H. Sundell, eds. *Milton and the Art of Sacred Song.* Madison, 1979.

Radzinowicz, Mary Ann. *Toward "Samson Agonistes": The Growth of Milton's Mind.* Princeton, 1978.

Rosenberg, D. M. *Oaten Reeds and Trumpets: Pastoral and Epic in Virgil, Spenser, and Milton.* Lewisburg, Pa., 1981.

Samuel, Irene. "The Development of Milton's Poetics." *PMLA,* XCII (1977), 231–40.

Steadman, John M. *Epic and Tragic Structure in "Paradise Lost."* Chicago, 1976.

Stein, Arnold. *The Art of Presence: The Poet and "Paradise Lost."* Berkeley, 1977.

Summers, Joseph H. *The Muse's Method: An Introduction to "Paradise Lost."* Cambridge, Mass., 1962.

Tayler, Edward W. *Milton's Poetry: Its Development in Time.* Pittsburgh, 1979.

Webber, Joan. *Milton and His Epic Tradition.* Seattle, 1979.

Wittreich, Joseph Anthony, Jr. *Visionary Poetics: Milton's Tradition and His Legacy.* San Marino, Calif., 1979.

Woodhouse, A. S. P. *The Heavenly Muse: A Preface to Milton.* Edited by Hugh MacCallum. Toronto, 1972.

INDEX

153